STANDARD CONTRACTS FOR BUILDING

GODWIN STUDY GUIDES

STANDARD CONTRACTS FOR BUILDING

DENNIS F. TURNER
B.A., F.R.I.C.S., M.C.I.O.B.
Construction Contracts Consultant

George Godwin

London and New York

George Godwin
an imprint of:
Longman Group Limited
Longman House, Burnt Mill, Harlow
Essex CM20 2JE, England
Associated companies throughout the world

*Published in the United States of America
by Longman Inc., New York*

© Dennis F. Turner 1984

First published 1984

British Library Cataloguing in Publication Data
Turner, Dennis F.
Standard contracts for building. — (Godwin study guides)
1. Joint Contracts Tribunal. Standard form of
building contract. 1980   2. Building — Contracts
and specifications — Great Britain.
I. Title
692′.8   TH425

ISBN 0-7114-5752-2

Library of Congress Cataloging in Publication Data
Turner, Dennis Frederick.
Standard contracts for building.

(Godwin study guides)
Bibliography: p.
Includes index.
1. Building — Contracts and specifications — Great
Britain.   I. Title.
KD1641.Z9T87   1984   34.41′07869   83-11670
ISBN 0-7114-5752-2 (pbk.)   344.1037869

Set in 10/11 pt Linotron 202 Times Roman
Printed in Hong Kong by
Commonwealth Printing Press Ltd

CONTENTS

CONTENTS

AN INTRODUCTION NOT TO BE IGNORED

Introductions are sometimes apologetic and sometimes anecdotal. This one aims to *introduce* this book and suggest how best to *use* it. Please read it!

The purpose is to act as a guide to the study of some of the standard contracts for building. It is intended for those taking examinations at degree, diploma, certificate, professional and technician level and for those in the construction industry seeking an introduction to such contracts or to bring their knowledge up to date. It is a *guide* to study of the contract themselves and in no way is it a substitute for reading the actual documents, which must be available therefore, but simply an attempt to ease such reading and explain what may not be apparent at first sight.

While this volume aims to highlight the main features and problems of the contracts considered, it does not elaborate on the finer points or make references to the legal cases that have led to or flowed from the wording of particular clauses, although a brief table of cases is given. Nor does it cover in detail more than the Joint Contracts Tribunal's standard form of building contract, mainly treating it in the private with quantities edition, indicating the differences in the variant editions and giving information on the related aspects of the sub-contract and supply documents. As well as these forms, there are specialised forms for other purposes which are listed in Chapter 2. For extended study, the reader is referred to the author's *Building Contract: a Practical Guide* which deals with these aspects and forms, among others, and also contains a bibliography of further wider reading.

The book has been structured in the following way and some comments on its use are given later:

Part 1. General principles. This sets out some key legal principles which apply to building contracts in general, without restricting them to the particular standard forms discussed in Part 2. It also outlines the principles of these standard forms.

Part 2. Contract clauses. Each chapter but the last takes the clauses of one particular form and groups them, so that a major set of topics is considered in a chapter. The arrangement of most chapters therefore follows a common pattern:
(*a*) *General considerations*: these are the principal elements in the clauses, discussed without close reference to wording or order

of the clauses so that the key issues may be picked out in advance of the detail.

(b) *Synopses of clauses*: these provide an outline of what the clause is saying, separately from comment and explanation. The summaries break down the often involved statements of the clauses into a series of short, structured elements. These should help to guide the reader, but inevitably they lose the precision and detail of the originals. It bears repetition already that they must not be read instead of the contracts, but alongside them.

(c) *Comments on clauses*: these are *selective* and pick out points *needing* comment, rather than just repeating what the clauses say. They must therefore be read in conjunction with the synopses and the contract wording. The comments do not always follow the order of the clauses, if it is more useful to group topics for discussion.

In several chapters this sequence of considerations, synopses and comments is repeated, so as to break the material of a related nature into manageable units. The last chapter is rather different and widens the subject to give a comparative treatment of the other forms mentioned in Part 1. They differ only in a few easily distinguishable respects.

Part 3. Contract themes. Here a radically different approach to the same material as in Part 2 is used. While that part of the book observes the clause structure, this part takes themes from the contract without any regard for the clauses as such. It thus traverses the same subject differently. Because principles and issues have already been discussed, this part consists largely of summary lists in the interests of brevity and to keep repetition to a minimum. It is not intended that these chapters should be fully intelligible without reference to those preceding them. They do however gather up threads which even a grouped clause approach does not emphasise. A closer introduction to them is given at the beginning of Part 3.

This arrangement should be useful to practitioners as giving a concordance enabling themes to be followed up in the contract and in the earlier parts of this book, thus providing an alternative to the usual alphabetical index also provided.

It is also intended that it should provide examination candidates with outline material for typical answers. It may be necessary to group material from several sections if a question is wide-ranging, and to reduce the amount of detail. The detail and discussion of the issues concerned is provided earlier in the book, and the outlines may be clothed accordingly. In relation to any one question, it would have been more simple to have produced a 'model' answer. This has not been done for several overlapping reasons: the same question may justify a different depth and length of answer in different examinations, there are so many possible questions (even if they are permutations and combinations of fewer basic points) and the precise emphasis of similar questions is important. In a subject like the present, the fairly rigid method of answering that is appropriate in, for instance, some mathematical work is quite inappropriate. The student must seek understanding of principles and then details, so that an answer is offered to the right question. A suitable range of actual examination papers will give the type of questions to be expected and these should suggest related questions on other aspects when set beside the outlines in Part 3.

In the light of all these points, a suitable order for study could be:

(a) Read lightly through Part 1 to appreciate its scope.

(b) Read the general considerations for any one chapter in Part 2 carefully and refer back to related sections in Part 1 more closely than before.

(c) Compare the actual contract clauses and the synopses of them in the same chapter.

(d) Follow with a close reading of the related comments to grasp the points discussed, but do not lose sight of the wording of the clauses or the synopses.

(e) Return to the general considerations and note how they work out in the details of the contract.

(f) Repeat (b)–(e) for each chapter in Part 2.

(g) Only then go on to Part 3, which may be studied in any order of themes.

Readers with a prior knowledge of the forms may well be able to vary the above. Indeed readers with enough background may find it suitable to start in Part 3 and work back to take the comments, etc. on a sampling basis. To help here, summaries of the chapters in Part 2 have been included in Chapter 12. These summaries may themselves also serve as outlines of examination answers. All of this gives a measure of repetition throughout the book to increase the number of 'signposts'.

Some remarks may be appended for examination candidates. This is *not* a book of examination techniques and certainly not one of short cuts: the subject needs application and thought. Selectivity is important so, as in any subject, do not clutter your answer with unwanted material – however fine it would be in answering another question! This is particularly true if you have the advantage of being allowed to refer to a copy of the contract during the examination. This becomes a disadvantage if you simply copy out great tracts cold. The examiner is interested in explanation and relevant concise references to the text of clauses to clarify this. But selectivity is not narrowness. A proper discussion may bring together several clauses and may draw in basic legal principles. Especially is this the case in dealing with questions that state problems or that are built around situations. Indeed here it may be what is *not* stated in the contract that is critical!

Lastly, here are some words to readers who seek knowledge for practical reasons alone. While the detail is kept to practical issues, discussion is conducted in the light of 'the letter of the law'. No doubt, it is often possible in practice to cut corners, have gentlemen's agreements, maintain goodwill or even be slipshod, and to simplify life in the process. One area where non-observance is false economy is over putting things in writing. The contracts require this so often that, to avoid tedium, it is not often repeated in either the synopses or the comments. Lack of written expression is the quickest way to confusion. Even more widely though, a book like the present can only base its discussion on 'the letter' and it is this that will be read (or its absence noted) in the unfortuate event of court action or reference to arbitration.

The whole matter of building contracts is becoming annually more intricate, as the forms, the legal proceedings and the available literature proliferate. It is hoped that this book will help at least some readers to acquire a basic knowledge of, if not a taste for, the subject-matter.

D.F.T.
June 1983

Part 1

GENERAL PRINCIPLES

CHAPTER 1

ASPECTS OF THE LAW AND BUILDING CONTRACTS

Before examining the standard forms of building contract considered in this book it is useful to survey in outline some of the legal principles that apply to standard forms in general. Their precise effect may well be qualified by the wording of the particular form, but a standard form cannot be read in isolation from them. The treatment is purely by way of summary and should be regarded as a series of signposts pointing to the world of legal reference books and living legal opinion. No summary can do more in a subject of such intricacy. Since other branches of the law often impinge on the affairs of a contract, that consideration is here limited to matters of contract law only should be sufficient warning.

The law of Scotland differs in important respects, not because it is a variant of English law, but because it derives from a different root. Under the Act of Union, it was enacted that Scotland should retain her distinctive legal system. The main reference is in English terms here, with differences noted.

THE BASIS OF A BUILDING CONTRACT

There is little about a building contract that is really distinctive legally when it is compared with other commercial contracts. The points that follow simply underline some of the more commonly relevant points.

Parties to the contract

There are only two parties to a building contract: the client or employer and the contractor, but due to the customary divisions of duties within the building process several other persons are usually named. Some of these are professional advisers to the employer, who are also given defined responsibilities and power under the contract. Nevertheless their only contract is with the employer and is quite independent of the building contract. Lapses on their part adversely affecting the contractor will usually, therefore, lead to action by the contractor against the employer, who may then have his own remedies against his advisers. Action by the contractor against the advisers is likely to arise in tort, if at all.

Other persons named in contracts are sub-contractors, so called because they have no privity of contract with the employer. They have, however, a normal contractual relation with the contractor. Their contracts may be affected by terms in the main building contract which are expressly referred to or which may be implied in particular circumstances. When a sub-contractor is nominated by the architect under the JCT form of main contract the sub-contract between him and the main contractor must be in the JCT standard form. When a sub-contractor is domestic, a standard form is available, but is optional.

Essentials of a valid contract

The features necessary to give a contract validity in court are often classed under six heads. Three of these heads need no expansion here:

(a) Intention to create legal relations.
(b) Genuine identity of consent as to the subject-matter.
(c) Capacity of the parties legally to enter into the contract.

The other three may be commented on as follows:

(d) *Offer and acceptance*. An invitation to tender is not an offer. The tender itself is the offer; this is true even if it is termed an estimate or if it amends some term of the invitation, such as the contract period or a description in the bills of quantities. An unqualified acceptance of a tender as submitted will constitute a binding contract, without the formal documentation which will follow. A qualified acceptance, including one that rejects any amendment to the terms of the invitation, is no acceptance and becomes a counter-offer awaiting acceptance in its turn. It follows from the next paragraph that an oral acceptance may be binding, if proved.

(e) *Form or consideration*. At least one of these two must be present in an English contract. Form in the legal sense exists where the contract is in writing and sealed by the parties. (This procedure is not available in Scotland, but a somewhat similar effect is produced by registration, should the parties wish to use it.) This type of contract is known as a contract under seal or a contract by deed or a speciality contract. It is a necessity in England where certain transactions in land are involved and where there is no consideration on one side of the contract, such as a contract to build without payment for the work. It used to be a necessity for corporations to contract under seal in most matters, but this was rendered optional for registered companies by the Companies Act 1948 and for other corporate bodies by the Corporate Bodies Contracts Act 1960. Government departments and statutory boards do not contract under seal. The major advantage of contracting under seal is that it secures a twelve-year right of action under the Limitation Act 1939; otherwise there is only six-year right.

Consideration is something of value promised by one party to the other in exchange for what the other promises. Normally this means the contract price on the one hand and the building works on the other, but some act, or even forbearance to act, by one party could constitute consideration. While consideration must be of some value, it need not match the consideration of the other party in value: the value can be quite minimal. A consideration which was entirely paid or performed before the contract was entered into is not however valid. In Scotland on the other hand a gratuitous promise is enforceable.

Any necessity of sealing a contract will make writing inevitable. Otherwise there is no necessity for a building contract to be in writing, although its usually complex terms will be difficult to prove if the contract is oral. It follows then that no particular form of words is obligatory and that a simple exchange of letters may suffice. The value placed on established wording is evidenced by the various standard forms available, however. A contract in writing and signed rather than sealed is known as a contract under hand.

(*f*) *Legality of object*. This mainly relates to absence of criminality in the intentions of the parties. As such, it is not lost by some accidental and incidental infringement of planning, building or licensing regulations; these are matters of means rather than ends. Such infringements could, however, lead to actions for damages by the injured party to the contract.

Implied terms in a building contract
There are circumstances in which a contract may be implied from the actions of the alleged parties and its terms deduced. Even when the existence of a contract is not in doubt, some of its terms may be. In the absence of express provisions, the following will be implied in a building contract:

(*a*) The employer will cause no delay or obstruction in giving or maintaining possession of the site or in furnishing information necessary to carry out and complete the work and will not improperly influence the architect, if there is one. He may not himself enter the site to do other work.

(*b*) The contractor will be workmanlike in both manner of execution and in quality of product and he will complete within a reasonable time.

(*c*) Both parties will agree to a reasonable price for the work.

In any work of consequence it is hoped that these terms will be expressed, as they are in the standard forms. In some cases, one party may contend that breach by the other or some other circumstance has subverted the express term and that a reasonable term should be implied. This will usually relate to time or price and if the contention is resisted it will need arbitration or legal action to resolve it.

Entirety

Most building contracts, including those related to standard forms of building contracts, are what is known as entire contracts. While many building contracts, including the standard forms, introduce modifications to the entire contract arrangement as is discussed under the next heading, they still remain entire contracts and it is useful to summarise the nature of such a contract. The key feature of an entire contract is that each party promises to the other a single consideration in return for the other's part. This usually means a whole payment by the employer for the whole work performed by the contractor. This may mean what is often termed a lump-sum contract where the employer's payment is fixed in advance and stated in the contract. The fact that the sum consists of several distinct parts adding up to the whole, or even of many items in a bill of quantities, does not modify this position. Further the contract remains entire if based on approximate quantities, a schedule of rates or prime cost; in these cases the basis of payment is defined, while the precise sum remains to be derived from the formula given. But the contract is still entire even if the price is not established in any way but simply implied; the oneness of the work to be performed and the oneness of the sum due are enough.

A contract will not be an entire contract where the contractor is not obliged to carry out the whole work specified and where the employer in turn may terminate the employment of the contractor when he chooses. A maintenance contract may be in this category by incorporating a break clause that either party may invoke.

Unless the terms of the contract modify matters, several things follow when a contract is entire, some of which may be mentioned:

(*a*) The contractor cannot claim any payment until he has completed the contract works. If he abandons the work he cannot claim payment for the part that he has carried out and indeed may be open to an action for damages. This will apply unless the failure to complete consists solely of the omission of some trivial item or items or unless the employer has prevented the contractor from completing the works.

(b) The contractor carries the whole risk of completion, even though the work is completely destroyed during progress and he has to re-execute it. He must do this without extra payment from the employer, although a reasonable extension of the time for completion would be allowed, even if not expressly envisaged in such circumstances. This position is however subject to frustration, as discussed below.

(c) The employer is bound to pay the whole price so soon as he is satisfied that the work is complete and he cannot hold any sum back against the possibility of defects. If these arise he will need to proceed in the usual ways for breach of contract.

(d) Neither party can oblige the other to accept any variations in the subject-matter of the contract. Thus the employer cannot require the contractor to do additional work, either on terms equivalent to those in the contract or on any other. While the employer reasonably may ask the contractor to forbear from executing part of the work, the contractor is not thereby obliged to agree to a reduction in the contract price. The contractor on his side obviously cannot expect unilaterally to vary the total amount of work, but further he cannot substitute one thing for another in any part and claim that the thing substituted is as good as, or even better than, the original. Any of these things can come about and be accepted only if the parties agree either in advance or after the event. The distinction between 'variations' and 'variation' is discussed under the heading of the latter below.

(e) Any work or materials which are reasonably necessary will be held to have been included in the contract price as being implied, even though not specifically mentioned.

Modifications

The above points give a fairly clear, but quite rigorous position. The standard forms all introduce terms which soften this, but do not cause the contract to cease to be entire. It is important to remember the underlying position when reading a standard form. Common modifications applicable to the forms discussed are:

(a) A right for the contractor to receive payment on account during progress, subject to a retention fund.

(b) A right of the employer to retain part of the fund for a period after completion, against the clearance of defects.

(c) The transfer of some risks from the contractor to the

employer, particularly regarding damage to the work; in addition there may be an obligation to insure, but this does not affect the basic contractual position regarding the contractor's risk.

(*d*) The recognition of the occurrence of some contingencies, including some matters under (*c*), as releasing the contractor from his obligation to complete.

(*e*) Rules governing forfeiture of the contract or determination of work under it by either party in various circumstances, including those under (*d*), and the payment of the contractor for the part of the work carried out.

(*f*) A right of the employer or his architect to require variations and rules governing how the contract price is to be adjusted.

While quantities as part of the contract do not destroy the entirety of a contract, they do produce a description of the work in considerable detail. There is a fine sub-division of the contract price, and that sub-division is regulated by detailed rules set out in the quantities or in an underlying standard method of measurement. These rules often mean that certain obligations must be stated in individual items or be made the subject of separate items, but they will not be implied if not stated. This produces a subtle but, in practice, very important modification of the general position that it is difficult to delineate precisely. The result is seen in many disputes in settling final accounts.

DISCHARGE AND CHANGE OF A BUILDING CONTRACT

Discharge

A building contract, like other contracts, may be discharged or brought to an end in a number of ways. The following are important in the general law:

(*a*) Performance. This is happily the most common ending.

(*b*) Waiver by one party, when he has completed his side of the agreement, of the outstanding obligations of the other party. This is probably the most uncommon ending, except over trivialities.

(*c*) Mutual agreement or abandonment of the work. This is sometimes termed an agreed recission.

(*d*) Unilateral recission. This may be upheld by the courts where one party discovers fraudulent misrepresentation by the other, such as the suppression of important known facts. It is not acceptable where statements are made as the 'best information available' or where it was impossible to know the facts in advance.

(*e*) Frustration. This must be some drastic occurrence of a quite unforeseeable business risk, such as prevention due to war or destruction of an existing building that is to be altered under the contract. A shortage of labour or material is not sufficiently drastic. Hindrance by the employer may be a sufficient ground, but only if the contractor cannot overcome it by exceptional measures, the most cost of which would be recoverable from the employer.

(f) Acceptance by one party of a breach by the other. This will usually need to be a fundamental breach or one that is laid down in the contract as sufficient. Such acceptance is termed forfeiture and is considered further below.

(g) Disclaimer by a trustee, receiver or the like where one party has become insolvent and the appropriate statute allows it (see 'Insolvency' below).

Breach
Forfeiture is the extreme remedy against breach, by which the injured party unilaterally ends the contract and proceeds against the other party to recover his loss. The contract may embody particular rules for calculating this loss, in which case the contract itself does not end at once, but the contractor's employment is determined and settlement follows. It may still be possible to go to arbitration or the courts for satisfaction in this latter case if the prescribed settlement is not adequate.

Since forfeiture is so extreme and usually applies only for fundamental breach, other remedies at law for breach will be followed where possible:

(a) Damages in respect of loss due to inadequate performance; liquidated damages are a particular variant and are discussed later in this chapter.

(b) An injunction restraining the commission of the breach.

(c) Specific performance to enforce the contract as intended; this is uncommon in building contracts because of the amount of detailed work involved.

Variation and rectification
A change of some term of a contract, such as the level of price or basis of payment or contract period, or a change of its scope, is termed variation of the contract. It must be evidenced in a manner of no less status than the original, which may have been oral, under hand or under seal.

Variation should be distinguished from variations which are incidental changes of detail within a contract, not changing its terms or scope. Variation must be specially agreed between the parties, while variations are authorised by the architect within the terms of the contract which gives him this limited power. It is necessary for an entire contract to be modified by a variations clause, as has been discussed, otherwise the architect has no power to introduce them or the employer to require them, and no terms for their valuation are available.

Where both parties have entered into a contract under a common misapprehension, it is obviously open to them to rectify their mistake by mutual agreement, much as they would effect variation of the contract. In general, if only one party has made a mistake he must stand by if it is to his detriment and the other party cannot insist that it is rectified if it has the opposite effect.

Assignment and sub-letting
Assignment is the unilateral passing over, by one party to a contract, of his part in it to another and is of several varieties, which are not distinguished in the standard forms. Broadly, while one party may often choose to perform a contract by the act of another, he may not in law assign it in such a way as to be relieved of the liability for performance. Standard forms usually restrict the right of a party to assign by making it subject to consent of the other. If such an agreed assignment involves the complete substitution of a new party for the old, it becomes novation, since a new contract has been created. Assignment by the employer presents fewer problems related to performance.

Sub-letting occurs when the contractor enters into a sub-contract with another firm for some part or even the whole of the work, while himself remaining in his existing relationship to the employer in all respects, including the receiving of instructions and payments. Usually sub-letting is of one trade or similar parcel of work at a time and it is made conditional upon consent or other control of the architect as the direct guardian of quality of work, but with withholding of consent made subject to arbitration.

SPECIAL PROVISIONS OF A BUILDING CONTRACT

Because of the nature of building work, the contracts used for its procurement usually embody a number of special procedural and other conditions. They may arise from the multiplicity of components in a building, the relatively long time required for their assembly, or simply from the fact that the contractor carries out the bulk of his work on someone else's land. Some of the main aspects of the leading conditions are discussed below.

Certificates

Certificates in standard forms of building contract serve three main purposes:

(a) To set out the architect's satisfaction with some aspect of the physical work and ultimately with the whole of it.

(b) To notify the employer that the contractor is entitled to payment, either interim or final.

(c) To embody the architect's decision as between the parties in some matter in which the contract gives him power.

Certificates serving the last purpose may be issued at various times and represent the architect's last word on the matters at issue. Certificates serving the other two purposes fall into two groupings: those issued during progress and those related to completion and what immediately follows. In general, these two groups do not indicate final agreement; they are not conclusive over the quality of work done, and they are only provisional on financial matters. It is only the final certificate that gathers up all the threads of a contract and gives conclusiveness.

Certificates may therefore also be classified as interim, completion and final. Of the first, no more need be said. The second group usually includes a certificate that the work is physically complete; while this does not indicate final satisfaction, it does end the contractor's liability to accept orders to perform any fresh work and, among other things, transfers responsibility for the care of the work from the contractor to the employer.

The final certificate ends the contract between the parties, although some liabilities under the Limitation Act will carry over. It is the architect's last word on quality, finance and any other issues. The certificate is usually declared by a standard form to be final and conclusive, subject to any outstanding matters referred to arbitration. While this is so, professional persons are not acting in a quasi-judicial capacity when preparing certificates. To be binding, the certificate must also be issued after fulfilment of any conditions precedent and there must not have been dishonesty on the part of the contractor or interference by the employer. The time for the issue of the final certificate is clearly specified in clause 30.8 of the JCT form, but the timetable there laid down is one of the least observed features of the contract.

Defective work

As mentioned earlier, a workmanlike product is at least an implied term in a building contract and in any reasonable contract there will be a description of the quality required. Usually the execution then has to be in conformity with standards that are generally recognised, such as standard specifications and codes of practice, and also to the reasonable satisfaction of the architect, which satisfaction is binding on the employer and contractor alike, subject to the right of one to go to arbitration against the other. In the latter case the architect's satisfaction is not simply an extra safeguard for the employer: it is the overriding term in respect of quality in the contract. While the architect's satisfaction has this binding effect on the two parties, the employer may still have a right of legal redress if the architect is negligent in exercising his duties to ensure that his satisfaction has been met. The extent of the architect's responsibility varies according to the provisions of the building contract and his own quite separate conditions of engagement.

The contractor is not liable for design or specification faults, unless his contract specifically makes him responsible for these aspects in any part of the work or unless an obligation to supplement aspects of a design can be implied, perhaps over complying with aspects of statutory regulations. This is a very intricate and poorly charted area of law and is becoming more so with advances of technology. It becomes even more troublesome where there is nomination of specialist firms who may be designing their own work in detail, so that the JCT pattern includes collateral agreements between the employer and the nominated firm to tie matters together. As a skilled person the contractor should, however, check the reasonableness and completeness of what he is asked to construct. He may otherwise have no redress if he carries out what was clearly wrong and then has to replace it, although if he is instructed to proceed after querying work he will not be liable for any resultant defect.

Under an unmodified entire contract, the contractor would be required to deliver up his work in accordance with the contract at completion. The standard forms modify this by giving the architect additional rights of inspection and condemnation during progress. Indeed if these were not provided much covered work would be impossible to test at completion and there would be no certainty of compliance. As it is, the contractor is liable to repair or to remove and replace during progress. The architect is not however obliged to find defects during progress and the contractor will still be liable if they are drawn to his attention at the end. It is after all a breach by the contractor if a defect is present at all.

A further modification at completion is the introduction of a defects liability period in the standard forms, obliging the contractor to make good defects that are his responsibility within a fixed period after completion. Under the Limitation Act the contractor would be liable for any breach, including one of workmanship, for a period of six or twelve years from its occurrence, according to whether the contract was under hand or under seal. The defects liability period runs for a much shorter period, usually six months, but during its currency adds to the statutory liability for damages the contractual liability to perform the actual remedial work without extra charge.

The final certificate in the JCT forms occurs after making good of defects and other named matters and ends the contract. It also expresses satisfaction with the work in such a way as to release the contractor from part of his burden under the Limitation Act. The period following the defects liability period and preceding the final certificate is the only period, therefore, during which the contractor's liabilities are neither more nor less than the Act provides.

To provide against the contractor not remedying defects himself, the standard forms introduce a right for the employer to engage others to do this upon the contractor's default and then to counter-charge the contractor. This can be done only after due notice to the contractor, since the cost may well be greater than if the contractor had done the work himself.

Liquidated damages

Liquidated damages may be defined as a provision in a contract, and therefore agreed between the parties to the contract at the time of entering into it, which aims to determine in advance the extent of the liability for some future, specified breach. They are to be distinguished from unliquidated damages which are ascertained after the breach. They are employed in a building contract mainly to deal with the contractor not completing the works by the agreed date and usually take the form of a sum of money. This sum becomes payable for each week or other declared period by which the completion date is overrun. The advantage of liquidated damages is that the payment for breach is settled within the contract and legal proceedings are avoided. In addition the contractor has a clearly measured incentive to meet his programme.

It is essential that the sum assessed should be reasonable in relation to the damage anticipated and to all known facts, even though precise calculation is not possible. Calculation should take account of loss of rent, interest or business, the cost of alternative accommodation or whatever factor is relevant to the project, making allowance for any expenses paid. The sum may thus vary considerably as a proportion of the capital cost, according to the purpose of the project, and is not related either directly to this capital cost or to the contractor's saving of outlay which he may achieve by letting a contract run over time. The contractor should be fairly aware of this purpose, otherwise he may justly dispute the amount of liquidated damages when they arise, on grounds of ignorance and so uncertainty about his liability.

If circumstances change during the contract period so that the actual damage incurred is greatly increased or decreased, there will not, however, be grounds for either party seeking a reassessment of the sum. It is the situation at the date of contract that is overriding.

The test of reasonableness is used to distinguish liquidated damages from a penalty. A penalty is a sum quite disproportionate to the employer's likely loss and is set at a punitive level to force completion on time. A penalty is unenforceable and the courts will review it on the application of the contractor and apply unliquidated damages. Again, if liquidated damages of the same amount are provided against the happening of any one of several events of differing magnitude, they will be set aside and normal damages applied, as one or more of the events should have attracted different amounts. What matters in distinguishing penalty and liquidated damages is the reasonableness of the amount; the use of either term is not in itself conclusive as to the nature of the sum.

There are several defences against the enforcement of a liquidated damages provision, among which are:

(a) The sum is really a penalty.

(b) There is no agreed date from which damages for non-completion will accrue.

(c) An extension of time has been granted.

(d) An extension of time has been granted unreasonably late.

(e) Extra work of consequence has been added into the contract.

(f) The employer has impeded the contractor.

(g) The employer has waived the completion date, expressly or by implication.

(h) There has been an early determination of the contract, preventing completion.

Of these, (a) and (b) have already been mentioned, while (e) to (h) call for no comment. A contract clause permitting extension of time is often regarded solely as a protection for the contractor against payment of damages. In addition, however, it protects the employer by keeping his rights to liquidated damages alive in the cases where the employer or his architect has caused the contractor's delay. Without such a clause the contractor would be entitled to substitute a reasonable amended completion date which

might well be somewhat later. But even when the right to liquidated damages is lost, the employer may still retain a right to
unliquidated damages in the normal way. It is generally the case
that the architect has to certify the amount of extension and that
he has to do this within a reasonable time of the cause of delay
arising. Sometimes this will mean before completion and sometimes not necessarily so, although it must always be as soon as is
practicable so that the contractor is not left in doubt over the date
and the intensity of effort that he needs to apply. The JCT form
has quite an elaborate procedure here.

Beyond those grounds for extension that arise out of default on
the employer's side, contracts contain some grounds such as
weather which are not the fault of either party and others over
which the contractor has some control. The tendency is for these
grounds to be widened progressively and thus limit the
contractor's risk and increase that of the employer.

Usually the architect will certify the actual completion date and
indicate that the original or some amended due completion date
should have been achieved. The employer may deduct damages
periodically from monies becoming payable so soon as the due
date is exceeded or he may ask the contractor to pay them to him.
His last opportunity under the JCT form is at the issue of the final
certificate.

It is sometimes contended that liquidated damages are not
enforceable unless there is a corresponding bonus payment
provided for early completion. This is not so, since they are a
payment for breach and not an allowance in respect of an adjustable term of the contract. A bonus payment balancing an apparent
penalty provision might well make the penalty enforceable, since
it would be evidence that the employer measured the value of
possession of his building in these terms.

Insolvency
The broad term insolvency is used throughout this book but there
are really two major divisions within it. In England a private
individual becomes bankrupt and his position is then regulated by
the Bankruptcy Act 1914; a company in similar unfortunate
circumstances goes into liquidation and its affairs are determined
under Part V of the Companies Act 1948. In Scotland the position
is broadly similar under different legislation. There are a number
of differences between the two cases which are beyond present
consideration, but in each case the philosophy is to bring the
affairs of the individual or company under the control of a
specially appointed receiver, trustee, manager or liquidator. This
person is charged with bringing affairs to an end in such a way as

to rescue from the shipwreck the maximum finances for distribution among the creditors as a whole. To this end he has power to carry on or disclaim contracts and dispose of assets and the like. The resulting final distribution will then be in proportion to the amounts owing to the various creditors, subject to any classes of them being entitled to prior satisfaction – such as debenture holders.

In building contracts there are few special problems if the employer becomes insolvent since his promised consideration is simply the payment of money. Where the contractor becomes insolvent the matter is more complex, since his consideration consists of the provision of a building and he may now fail to continue with it when it is standing in a far from finished state. If he or someone on his behalf does complete the work, then affairs are straightforward contractually. To provide for cessation of work due to the one party's insolvency, standard forms incorporate a number of provisions. Since several of these attempt to give the solvent party preferential treatment as against the rest of the creditors, they may be invalid at law, according, perhaps, to whether the contractor is an individual or a company. The main subjects to which these provisions relate are:

(*a*) Establishment of retention monies as trust funds. This may be done for retention held on the contractor's or sub-contractors' work when the employer becomes insolvent or on that of sub-contractors when the contractor becomes insolvent. While this may be legally sound against the claims of other creditors, it may fail in practice if the monies are not held in a distinctly constituted and identifiable fund, as the JCT form provides may be set up.

(*b*) The right of the contractor's trustee or the like to proceed or disclaim. This right is given for the overall benefit of the creditors as a whole and stipulations that the employer is to have an overriding option of determination are likely to be unsound if challenged.

(*c*) The ownership of materials and plant on site. An unequivocal provision that these items vest in the employer simply by being brought on to the site is effective before the contractor's insolvency and is therefore not disturbed by it, provided that they are already the property of the contractor. A lesser provision, such as that they are 'deemed to vest' in the employer, or that he may have the use of them until completion of work, will give no effective ownership unless the items are also paid for in interim payments. Under the JCT pattern, materials are used after insolvency and in effect paid for in the final settlement, while plant is used without payment and then returned to the contractor. Materials to which the contractor does not have a good title do not pass to the employer even when paid for under interim payments, while in no case will hired items pass to the employer by virtue of terms written into a contract to which the hirer is no party.

(*d*) The ownership of materials not on site. On insolvency an individual or company will be held to be the reputed owner of such materials as are in his control with an apparent right of disposal, and thus these materials will be available to the trustee or the like. Provisions may therefore be introduced to establish ownership by the employer of materials paid for but not on site, with requirements about identification and so forth. These may be effective where the contractor is a company, but may be weak where he is an individual. They are in any case ineffective in Scotland in this form, as indicated in Chapter 12.

When the contractor's insolvency is accompanied by some breach giving rise to determination, such as lack of progress, the employer may find that determination on this other ground is better for him if he does not wish to retain the contractor. Since even an insolvent contractor or his trustee or the like is still under normal contractual obligations, such a determination would be quite enforceable. It does not help the position over the other matters, however.

CHAPTER 2

STANDARD FORMS OF CONTRACT

This chapter surveys a particular group of standard forms, while
noting the existence of others, and sets out the principles of those
forms out of the group which are considered in the rest of this
book. Like any other legal documents, such forms need a careful
approach in several ways:

(*a*) They must be read in the light of the relevant law which
bears upon their interpretation. Seldom do clauses in a contract
say everything about the points that they cover, and often they
import or exclude a whole area of principles. Sometimes they run
counter to some legal principle which the parties cannot exclude,
even by agreement, possibly because to do so would be to conflict
with public interest. Such reasons account for the presence of
Chapter 1.

(*b*) They must be read in the light of any other contract document. The forms in question are drafted to go with clearly distinguished documents and they define fairly closely how all the
documents relate to each other. Especially they state which document overrides another in the event of a clash of meaning or
content. Sometimes relationships have to be inferred. In any case,
a clear view of the demarcations is critical.

(*c*) They must be read in the light not only of practical operations when 'everyone knows what is wanted', but of the possibility
of disagreement between the client and the contractor as the
contracting parties. A number of potential hazards are anticipated
and ways of overcoming them are provided in the forms, usually
requiring the architect or occasionally the quantity surveyor to sort
out the details. Contracts do not provide for all eventualities,
however, and there is always the possibility of a petulant party
seeking legal proceedings against the other party, even when there
are applicable clauses, possibly to attempt to secure a reversal of
the decision of architect or quantity surveyor.

STANDARD FORMS IN GENERAL

Some clients and some contractors in the construction industry
have their own individually prepared forms of contract which they

put forward to the other party and which are only 'standard' in that they are used regularly by their authors. These forms usually have some particular emphasis related to the type of work or its method of procurement. Being the work of one party, they frequently have some particular emphasis in allocating contractual responsibilities and risks. The other party, if discerning, may not therefore enter into one of these contracts without some amendment to its terms. Such a policy of particular contract forms is especially common in industrial engineering construction, as well as in specialised areas of building and civil engineering.

Otherwise there are several groups of contracts which represent consultation or agreement between representatives of clients and contractors from the sector of the industry concerned. These contracts have been prepared to meet a range of projects and methods of obtaining them. As such, they can be used as they stand, subject to choosing from a few alternative clauses and to filling in spaces in appendices and the like to give specific amounts of time and money and other individual elements for the project concerned. Occasionally it may be necessary to make some unscheduled change to the conditions as printed. In view of the close interrelation of many clauses and the danger of introducing an unintended meaning, ambiguity or even nonsense, such changes should be avoided whenever possible. If they cannot be avoided, specialist legal advice should be sought.

Three groups of forms may be mentioned, these being the main strains available for contracts of all sizes. Several forms of other origins are in use, and these usually aim for the smaller projects or at least to be less complex in wording. The three groups, of which only the first is considered further in this volume, are:

(a) The Joint Contracts Tribunal (JCT) forms: these are produced by a body of representatives from various and quite different constituent bodies and are the result of consensus, although some of the bodies have reservations over particular emphases in the documents. They are intended solely for building work, but there is quite a range of forms for various purposes. This range is described in the next section of this chapter, along with a number of related forms prepared by some of the constituent bodies.

(b) The Institute of Civil Engineers (ICE) forms: these are produced between the various bodies of consultant and contracting engineers and are the result of consensus, with few misgivings. There are main and sub-contract forms, intended solely for civil engineering work. The only financial basis is approximate quantities and remeasurement and the forms are mainly used by public bodies, although they can be used by private clients. There are derived forms for use in international civil engineering contracting.

(c) The central government forms, the primary one usually being known briefly (its title is quite long) as Form GC/Works/1: these are produced within the departments concerned, but in consultation with contractors' representatives. They are not therefore consensus documents, although not entirely unilateral products. Form GC/Works/1 is a good-tempered document that can be used for building and civil engineering work, on the basis of drawings and specification, firm or approximate quantities or a schedule of rates. There are related forms for engineering services and for minor works.

JCT GROUP OF STANDARD FORMS

This book discusses the most commonly used of the JCT series, and especially those under (a) below, but the whole series is reviewed below. Most of them are in their 1980 editions. These represent either a complete revision of the previous documents or fresh documents introduced in restructuring the series as a whole. From time to time, revisions of what will still be called the '1980 editions' may be expected.

(a) *Standard form of building contract*: this is intended for the traditional arrangement of architect design and contractor construction. It is in three parts, with the first two in one binding and the third separately. Part 1 covers the general clauses and Part 2 covers nominated work and these are issued in six variants:

Private with quantities
Private with approximate quantities
Private without quantities
Local authorities with quantities
Local authorities with approximate quantities
Local authorities without quantities

Part 3 covers fluctuations and is issued in two variants, private and local authorities, within each of which are alternatives for quantities, approximate quantities and without quantities. This contract is outlined in more detail in the last section of this chapter and is then analysed and discussed in the rest of this book. The other contracts listed below under (d), (e) and (g) follow its general structure and detail as far as possible.

(b) *Sectional completion supplement to the standard form*: this is available in one version to go with any of the six foregoing and consists entirely of amendments to allow phased completion of the works to be written into the contract. It is referred to in the present text at appropriate points.

(c) *Addendum to the standard form with quantities and contractor's proposals*: this is rather larger than a supplement, but again amends the standard form to introduce design of *part* of the works by the contractor. There are variants for quantities, approximate quantities and without quantities. This and the next three versions are not discussed in this book.

(d) *Standard form of building contract with contractor's design*: this document is available in one form for private and local authorities use and puts *all* design responsibility with the contractor, so that an architect does not figure in its clauses. It is a completely self-contained document and in essence based upon a lump sum with drawings and specification.

(e) *Fixed fee form of prime cost contract*: this again is a private or local authorities document. It is based upon architect design, but the basis of payment is related to costs as incurred by the contractor, rather than priced quantities or a lump sum.

(f) *Agreement for minor building works*: this is issued in private and local authorities versions and is quite short and intended for quite small drawings and specification projects.

(g) *Nominated sub-contract forms*: there are two versions of the sub-contracts themselves, divided into two parts for general clauses and fluctuations clauses. They are almost identical but related to whichever of the two methods of nomination is employed. Either may be used with any of the main standard forms under (a) above and both may occur under the same main contract. They permit firm or approximate quantities, a schedule of rates or a simple lump-sum basis. Both have a related but separate form of employer/nominated sub-contractor agreement and one has a related form of tender and form of nomination. All of these documents and the methods of nomination are considered in relation to the main contract in Chapter 5 and at other points in the text.

(h) *Nominated supplier forms*: there are two forms here, a form of tender with warranty agreement and a form of nomination. They are for use with the forms under (a) above and again are mentioned in Chapter 5.

STANDARD FORMS RELATED TO THE JCT GROUP

Two distinct types are involved here and have been produced by constituent bodies of the JCT to dovetail with the Tribunal's own forms.

(*a*) *National Federation of Building Trades Employers domestic sub-contract form*: this is published in one version and is equivalent to the JCT nominated sub-contracts in purpose and identical where applicable in content. It is not obligatory to use it within the overall scheme, although desirable for the larger sub-contracts. No form of tender is published. The form does not need separate discussion in the text.

(*b*) *Scottish Building Contract Committee forms*: these are necessary because Scotland has a separate legal system. Only the prime cost contract out of the JCT series is drafted to be used as it stands in Scotland. For the main and sub-contract forms a 'conditions only' version is available, that is one without the articles of agreement and the appendix (see the next section of this chapter). There are separate Scottish building contracts (including a sectional completion variant) and Scottish building sub-contracts which contain sections equivalent to the articles of agreement and appendix, set out a number of amendments to the JCT conditions and incorporate the 'conditions only' document by reference. In the case of sub-contract and supplier forms of tender, employer agreement forms and nominated forms, complete Scottish documents are issued. There are also two extra contracts of purchase not corresponding to any JCT documents. The principal differences introduced by the contracts, sub-contracts and contracts of purchase are outlined at the end of Chapter 11.

PRINCIPLES AND STRUCTURE OF JCT STANDARD FORM OF BUILDING CONTRACT

All six variants of the form are modified entire contracts of the general type described in Chapter 1. In particular they are all lump-sum contracts, even though the lump sum may be based on firm quantities which can be varied or, even more, although the lump sum is not ascertained until after complete remeasurement of approximate quantities. These and other modifications of the entirety principle are noted in respect of the clauses concerned in later chapters.

The client under the contract is known as the employer, who is given a largely passive role. The contractor, as the other party, interacts on most issues with the architect who is frequently mentioned throughout the conditions. The latter is in his traditional role as designer engaged under a separate contract by the employer, so that among his responsibilities under the present contract is that of seeing that his design is implemented by the contractor. But in addition to acting in this way for the employer, he also has several duties under this contract in which he has to act and decide between the parties. Whatever powers and duties the contract assigns him, he must in any case perform them impartially and on the basis of a considered interpretation of the contract in all its parts, without being influenced by the employer. If either party objects to his actions the remedy, as mentioned earlier, is to seek arbitration or court action. This must be against the other party and *not* against the architect himself, as he is not a party to the contract.

The quantity surveyor in principle is in a similar position to the architect under the contract, but he is mentioned much less often and his role is a more passive one of settling up financially and not of controlling events. Even here, he is dependent on the architect's decisions and delegation over a number of matters.

While the form in each variant is issued in the two documents already mentioned, it consists functionally of four sections:

Articles of agreement
Conditions
Appendix
Supplemental provisions

The first three of these are defined by the conditions as separate contract documents, alongside the contract drawings and contract bills. The last of the four contains the VAT agreement which needs to be considered no further.

The articles of agreement state several salient features, particularly the names of the parties to the contract, the title and site of the work, the other contract documents, the contract sum and the names of architect and quantity surveyor. They also contain the arbitration agreement.

The conditions are the most substantial section and are made up of what are known individually as clauses. Discussion of these occupies most of this book. There are a few places where optional or alternative wording or clauses exist and it is necessary to delete the unwanted versions. There are no places requiring insertions of specific contract details in the conditions themselves. Instead there are quite a number of references to the appendix which consists of a schedule of points requiring completion, such as the contract dates, the level of damages, the frequency of payment certificates and the level of retention. These elements are discussed under the clauses that refer to them.

Provided that the articles of agreement and the appendix are filled in and that the options and alternatives in the conditions are dealt with, these three contract documents will be complete and consistent, whether they say what is actually wanted or not! It is regular practice when bills of quantities in accordance with the Standard Method of Measurement (SMM) are used for tendering, to give notice in the preliminaries of what is proposed for all of these variable elements. This action is however only indicative, even though the bills become a contract document, and all of the points must be dealt with in the formal copy of the JCT form to be effective. It is sometimes the practice also to amend or amplify contract clauses by wording in the preliminaries. Here again, the wording must be incorporated into the formal document to be effective, as indicated in Chapter 3. Whether it is wise to use such wording at all is another issue.

Within the conditions, the clauses in Part 1 follow an order that broadly represents general matters, the order of normal events and possible mishaps and some appended matters. The order is difficult to understand in places (e.g. why completion precedes commencement) and does not always suit the type of introduction that this book offers. Parts 2 and 3 of the conditions also bear relating to elements in Part 1. For these reasons, the discussion chapters in Part 2 of this book take the clauses rearranged in groups to suit the immediate purpose. Part 3 of this book deals with topics that extract references from the clauses and arrange them into quite different structures, so that study may proceed by various routes.

Apart from anything already written and incidental references hereafter, the following sections of the JCT form are *not* considered specifically in this book:

Articles of agreement, other than the arbitration provision (see Ch. 15)
Clause 15. Value added tax – supplemental provisions
Clause 31. Finance (No. 2) Act 1975 – statutory tax deduction scheme
Supplemental provisions (the VAT agreement)

All but the last chapter of Part 2 summarise and comment upon the form in its private with quantities variant. The last chapter of Part 2 comments upon the main differences in the other five variants and in the Scottish forms.

Part 2
CONTRACT CLAUSES

CHAPTER 3

SCOPE AND CARRYING OUT OF THE WORKS

GENERAL CONSIDERATIONS

The earlier clauses of the conditions are concerned with matters of general applicability rather than with those relating to particular stages of the works or to infrequent occurrences. Among the major themes are the works themselves and the documents portraying them, the financial basis and the roles of architect and contractor. The general philosophy may be outlined:

(*a*) The architect is entirely responsible for designing and specifying the works and the contractor has no responsibility or right to perform these functions. There is no mention in the contract of consultants and in the present context they must be regarded as subsumed within the architect.

(*b*) The contractor is entirely responsible for organising the activity of construction and for the programme, methods and changes to produce the finished works in accordance with the design and specification. Any limitations on his approach must be laid down in the documents.

(*c*) The design and specification are embodied in the contract drawings and contract bills and so communicated to the contractor. They may be amplified, but not amended, by detail drawings, schedules of data, setting out information etc. issued by the architect post-contractually. They may be modified by him to resolve internal discrepancies in general and those with statutory obligations in particular, and also by various types of instructions issued by the architect. One of the most important types is that of design changes or variations, as considered in Chapter 9.

(*d*) The works as they progress and at completion are verified by the architect as according with the contract. To this end he has rights of access, of inspection and of acting through other persons. He may approve or condemn work, although he need not do so at an early stage.

(*e*) The contract sum is fixed when the contract is entered into and may not be set aside in favour of some other basis of payment. It may however be adjusted for reasons specifically given in the conditions, but not otherwise. A number of these reasons occur in the present group of clauses and they are all listed in Chapter 15.

The comments on matters in the clauses, following the synopsis, are arranged according to several themes rather similar to the foregoing and not in clause order.

SYNOPSIS OF CLAUSES 1–12, 14

CLAUSE 1: INTERPRETATION, DEFINITIONS ETC.
1.1 ● Reference method for clauses
1.2 ● Documents to be read as whole
1.3 ● Definitions of words/phrases with capital initials in documents

CLAUSE 2: CONTRACTOR'S OBLIGATIONS
2.1 ● Contractor to execute works
    ● subject always to conditions
    ● as contract drawings and contract bills
    ● otherwise to architect's satisfaction
2.2 ● Conditions override if any conflict
    ● Contract bills based on SMM6
    ● errors etc. treated as variations
2.3 ● Discrepancies in documents to be resolved by architect's instructions

CLAUSE 3: CONTRACT SUM – ADDITIONS OR DEDUCTIONS – ADJUSTMENT
             – INTERIM CERTIFICATES
    ● If contract sum adjustable according to conditions
        ● to be done in interim payments as soon as possible

CLAUSE 4: ARCHITECT'S INSTRUCTIONS
4.1 ● Contractor to comply with instructions
    ● otherwise others brought in to do work concerned
4.2 ● But only become instructions when shown to be in accordance with conditions
4.3 ● Instructions to be in writing or confirmed
    ● as timetable given, or
    ● before final certificate issued

CLAUSE 5: CONTRACT DOCUMENTS – OTHER DOCUMENTS – ISSUE OF
             CERTIFICATES
5.1 ● Custody of contract documents by architect/quantity surveyor
5.2 ● Copies of contract documents for contractor

5.3 • Supplementary post-contract information
     • schedules for contractor
     • master programme for architect (optional)
5.4 • Amplifying drawings and details to contractor
5.5 • Documents to be kept on works
5.6 • Return of documents finally
5.7 • Limitations on use of documents
5.8 • Architect's certificates to be sent to employer
     • with copy to contractor

CLAUSE 6: STATUTORY OBLIGATIONS, NOTICES, FEES AND CHARGES
6.1 • Contractor to comply with statute
     • notice to be given to architect of discrepancies
     • architect to resolve and issue any instruction
     • limited emergency action to be taken by the contractor and architect informed
     • contractor absolved if follows foregoing procedure
6.2 • Contractor to pay fees etc. and indemnify employer over same
     • Amounts to be added to contract sum, unless covered
     • as nomination
     • already in contract bills
       • by pricing
       • by provisional sum
6.3 • Work by body under statutory obligations *not* to be sub-contract

CLAUSE 7: LEVELS AND SETTING OUT OF THE WORKS
     • Architect to supply levels and setting out drawings for contractor to set out works
     • contractor responsible for cost of amending errors
     • unless architect instructs otherwise

CLAUSE 8: MATERIALS, GOODS AND WORKMANSHIP TO CONFORM TO
          DESCRIPTION, TESTING AND INSPECTION
8.1 • Materials etc. to be as contract bills
8.2 • Vouchers to prove this, if requested
8.3 • Architect may instruct opening up or testing of *any* work or materials
     • cost to be added to contract sum, unless
       • included in contract bills, or
       • results adverse
8.4 • Architect may instruct removal of defective work or materials
8.5 • Architect may instruct exclusion of persons employed

CLAUSE 9: ROYALTIES AND PATENT RIGHTS
9.1 • Royalties etc. included in contract sum
   • contractor to indemnify employer over claims etc.
9.2 • If resulting from architect's instructions
   • contractor not to indemnify employer
   • amounts of royalties, claims etc. added to contract sum

CLAUSE 10: PERSON-IN-CHARGE
   • Persons-in-charge to be constantly on works, to receive instructions

CLAUSE 11: ACCESS FOR THE ARCHITECT TO THE WORKS
   • Architect and representatives to have right of access to
   • works
   • workplaces etc. including those of sub-contractors

CLAUSE 12: CLERK OF WORKS
 (• Clerk of works (appointed by employer) to act solely as inspector
   • under directions of architect
   • his own directions must be confirmed as architect's instructions

CLAUSE 14: CONTRACT SUM
14.1 • Quality and quantities of work in contract to be as in contract bills
14.2 • Contract sum to be fixed
   • except when conditions allow adjustment
   • errors of pricing (but not of quantities) *not* adjustable

COMMENTS ON CLAUSES 1–12, 14

No points of substance arise over clause 1, once it is noted that it is concerned with basic definitions relating to the contract and with a number of detailed definitions which are discussed as necessary under the clauses in which they occur. Straightforward practical points about documents are covered in clauses 5.1, 5.2, 5.5, 5.6 and 5.7 and need no comment. All other clauses, to the level of the first decimal sub-divisions, are mentioned in the following groupings.

Documents and information
Clause 2.1 defines the contract documents as those documents under discussion in this book, and also the contract drawings and

contract bills. These latter define the works physically and establish what the contract is about and the detail of it. Nothing more is said in the conditions about the status of the contract drawings, their general function being fairly self-evident. In the case of the contract bills, there are several points. There is more scope in a largely verbal document for a clash with the conditions etc. and so in the first place clause 2.2.1 provides that these latter shall prevail in such a case. The possibility of a difference is strongest in the bill preliminaries, containing as they do stipulations over responsibilities and the like. If the difference has occurred accidentally, clause 2.2.1 produces the desired correction. It is not infrequent, however, for requirements to be included deliberately which purport to 'override or modify' the contract conditions. If so, the conditions as included in the formalised contract must be directly amended to take in these requirements, otherwise they will be nullified by the present clause. Only if a requirement supplements without modifying (and this is a very difficult thing to achieve) can it be included in the bills alone. In most cases it is better to play safe and duplicate the wording.

Clause 14.1 establishes the bills as giving 'the quality . . . of the work', so that they embody the specification detail mentioned in clause 2.1. This leaves any specification notes included on the drawings as having no contractual significance, unless they have been incorporated into the bills at least by reference. Clause 8.1 backs up these two clauses by referring to the contract bills for 'kinds and standards': this seems to be purely for good measure. The only fresh point is 'so far as procurable' which protects the contractor against having to obtain the unobtainable, but does not say what is to be done next. A request by the contractor for a variation may perhaps be inferred.

Clause 14.1 also establishes the bills as giving 'the . . . quantity of the work included in the Contract Sum'. This does not act as a strait-jacket on how much work the contractor is to do, but it does give the basis of the contract sum. The contract bills may be in error, giving an erroneous basis, and clause 2.2.2 deals with this.

The two parts of clause 2.2.2 take two questions. The bills are in accordance with SMM6, so that the contractor knows the precise rules followed when he tenders. Any departure from the rules must be expressed quite categorically in the bills, both as to its nature and which items are affected. This leads to the question of errors in the bills, defined as a departure from SMM6 (and presumably undisclosed) or a straightforward descriptive or quantitative mistake. The importance of identifying departures from SMM6 is clear. As the contract sum is based on whatever is in the contract bills, the provision for correcting the bills and so adjusting the contract sum is only fair. No variation instruction is required and the quantity surveyor can act when he alone has decided the matter. It is more than conjecture that this provision is often used to take up aberrations in quantities included in 'firm' bills in the absence of detailed drawings. None of these adjustments is due to any error in the prices and arithmetic in the contract bills and clause 14.2 forbids anything being done on this score.

The wider question of error among the contract documents and some documents issued post-contractually is taken in clause 2.3 over 'discrepancy or divergence'. This type of error is something apparent when the documents are worked through carefully and not something hidden, as the errors in the bills just mentioned may be. It is apparent because two or more statements, however given, are in conflict and so the contractor may be uncertain as to which to follow. Even if he thinks he knows the explanation, he must refer the matter to the architect for clarification. The consequent architect's instruction may then result in a variation and price adjustment.

The documents issued post-contractually include instructions and these are dealt with in various places in this book. Lists of the various types of instructions are given in Chapter 13. Most of them do not introduce changes in the works as do variation instructions, which are therefore excluded from the scope of clause 2.3.3. The other documents are intended simply to clarify to the contractor in detail what he has to do, work which is already included in the contract bills and so in the contract sum, but which does not show explicitly in the bills or on the drawings. These documents thus should introduce no change and are:

(a) Descriptive schedules, such as a schedule of room finishes, under clause 5.3.1.1.

(b) Further drawings or details, the extent of which will depend on the contract drawings, under clause 5.4.

(c) Levels and setting out information, the latter restricted to information at ground level to relate the works to the site, so that the contractor may perform the actual levelling and setting out under clause 7.

All of these are variously described as 'necessary' or 'required' for the contractor to work. Only in the case of the first is it made explicit by clause 5.3.2 that the information is to impose nothing extra on the contractor, but the point is implicit in the other cases. If the architect wishes to introduce some change when issuing any of this information it may be most simple to do so as an integral part of it. Provided he covers the change in an accompanying variation instruction, the position should be clear, even if the sequence does not satisfy the pedant. In the case of the clause 7 information, what is supplied is sufficiently fundamental for the point to be made explicit that the contractor is to amend errors at his own cost. This is true of all the work that the contractor performs, from the wrong colour of paint on a door to the overall height of the building, but it is not said clearly anywhere else except about defects in clause 17. It follows more widely from the obligation in clause 2.1 on the contractor to carry out the works in accordance with the contract standards.

A last type of document introduced in these clauses is the certificate. Clause 5.8 sets out the procedure by which the architect issues it to the employer, but with a copy to the contractor. Often the employer has to act on the certificate but the contractor needs warning, perhaps to take some independent action. The various certificates mentioned in the conditions are listed in Chapter 13.

Contractor's actions

The overriding responsibility of the contractor contained in clause 2.1 is to 'carry out and complete the Works', so repeating what is in the articles of agreement. As has been indicated at the beginning of the chapter, this is a construction and not a design responsibility. It is however a heavy responsibility legally by virtue of the 'entire contract' basis of this contract, even though it is lightened by a number of provisions (see Ch. 1). Clause 2.1 is so critical as to warrant emphasising its main statements as follows:

(*a*) The responsibility is to carry out *and complete*, so that the contractor is bound to complete, almost however onerous this may become, and he is held to the requirements in the contract over time and other intangible matters. Once he has completed though, he cannot be required to undcrtake any further new work.

(*b*) The works are those comprised within the contract documents, neither more nor less. This means a contract of defined character and extent. It is not possible for the employer to insist that a radically different type of building be substituted or that the size be doubled. Neither can the contractor opt out of half of the works.

(*c*) Both these statements are to be read as 'subject to the Conditions', which do allow the contractor *inter alia* not to complete in some circumstances and which allow the architect to issue various instructions, including some introducing variations and other limited changes.

(*d*) The quality of what is performed is to be in accordance with the contract documents, or where stated to the architect's satisfaction. This is to be 'reasonable', so that the contractor has the option of arbitration (see Ch. 15) if he considers he is being hard done by. If nothing is said about standard there would still be a presumption of a reasonable standard.

In addition to the contractor having this static picture of what he must achieve, he also has to comply with the architect's instructions which may introduce changes in various ways. Clause 4 regulates the procedure over instructions and is discussed more fully under the architect's actions below. A list of matters on which instructions may be given is included in Chapter 13. The contractor is protected by the clause in two ways against any arbitrary use of the power to instruct: he has a right to challenge whether an instruction is of a type permitted by the conditions, and all instructions must be in writing to be valid (like many other things in the conditions) and therefore definite in content. The contractor may confirm back to the architect any oral communication. This is expressed as a duty by the clause, but until and unless the instruction is confirmed it is not effective. If nothing happens by way of confirmation or compliance matters may simply lapse.

The only document which the contractor may be required to supply to the architect is his master programme under the optional clause 5.3.1.2. This programme is to be revised to take account of any extension of time granted by the architect, but this does not extend to revisions due to the contractor changing the programme for other reasons. Since the programme has no contractual effect by virtue of clause 5.3.2, the contractor is at liberty to change it when he will, so long as he observes the completion date and any intermediate dates given in the contract. Furnishing the programme is presumably meant to give the architect a guide on his programme for supplying information to the contractor, although it does not absolve the contractor from requesting any information in detail to satisfy clause 25.4.6. The programme may also be used by the quantity surveyor for a cash-flow forecast.

The primary responsibility for complying with statutory requirements, operating the associated routines and making payments, rests with the contractor under clauses 6.1.1 and 6.2. These requirements are 'with regard to the Works', that is the construction aspects, and so do not extend to matters like planning permission which are for the employer and the architect to clear. Not all of the contractor's obligations will be evident from the contract documents, for example matters of safety, and he rather than the employer is liable for complying with all such performance obligations without qualification. When however the contract documents or a variation instruction show a particular way of satisfying a statutory requirement, for example over a constructional detail, the possibility of a divergence exists. As the contractor has to satisfy two masters here, architect and statute, he is to refer any problem that he finds to the architect under clause 6.1.2 for an instruction. Any divergence coming to the architect's attention by this or any other means is to be resolved or lead initially to a holding instruction under the timetable of clause 6.1.3, while any action by the contractor to comply with statute in an emergency is to be ratified under clause 6.1.4.

Provided that the contractor plays his part by giving notice of any divergence that he finds, he is not liable by virtue of clause 6.1.5 for any residual non-compliance with statute. This relieves him of any absolute obligation to find all divergences, although there may be room for doubt on occasions as to whether he should have found something.

The contractor is also responsible as indicated above for payment of fees and charges arising. Clause 6.2 divides these into two classes: those which are to be added to the contract sum, that is be an extra on the contract, and those which are not. They are all regarded as extra unless they fall into the types listed, for each of which the contract bills must have made some form of provision, even if there is then to be adjustment. It is possible to include an omnibus item for pricing by the contractor in the contract bills covering all fees and charges, in which case no extra or adjustment would occur. The intention of such an item must be made quite clear. Clause 6.3 contains a definition that causes uncertainty about the status of such work which is outside the immediate discussion. This is mentioned again in Chapter 4.

The particular responsibility of the contractor to work from any levels and setting out information provided by the architect, has already been mentioned and needs no elaboration.

The contractor will wish to supervise the works for his own purposes. Clause 10 goes further and requires a person-in-charge for ease of communication. He does not have any greater delegated authority under the contract, and the contractor would need to make any delegation express.

Architect's actions
These may be summarised as supplying information, resolving problems over information already supplied and checking that all is going on in accordance with the contract. His lack of power to order the contractor's affairs has already been mentioned. He has numerous other rights and duties on other matters under the conditions, beyond those now considered (see Ch. 13).

The information which the architect has to supply has been discussed in most cases, but may be summarised as follows:

(*a*) The contract documents, with further copies of contract drawings and bills of quantities.

(*b*) Supplementary information by way of levels and setting out, descriptive schedules and detail drawings.

Failure on the first score is a breach on the part of the employer, while failure on the second may lead to an extension of time or a loss and expense payment. In a drastic case, a contractor may be able to determine his own employment. (See clauses 25, 26 and 28.)

Other information which the architect is almost bound to supply is by way of instructions under clause 4. The contractor's relationship to these has already been mentioned. The matters on which the architect has power to instruct are limited to those listed under 'Architect' in Chapter 13. These may be divided broadly into several categories:

(*a*) Matters on which the architect must act to permit progress, such as nominations and provisional sums.

(*b*) Matters on which the architect should act to ensure that the contract can be and is fulfilled by the contractor, such as defects and divergences.

(c) Matters on which the architect may choose to act or be required to act by the employer, such as variations and postponement.

Several issues flow from the power to issue instructions. The contractor may neglect to comply with an instruction, in which case the architect may give him a reminding notice under clause 4.1.2 to comply and then, if necessary, the employer may bring other persons to do the piece of work and secure the various costs from the contractor. This is alternative to the drastic remedy of determination open to the employer and available in more serious circumstances. It is intended for discrete parcels of work, including the removal of defective work, and can arise only as the result of instructions and not over failure to perform work included in the original contract. It is something that could not be done without this clause, since it would infringe the contractor's exclusive possession of the site, and that must not be done until the instruction is properly issued.

The other issues are those mentioned earlier as protecting the contractor over whether an instruction is properly issued by being valid in nature and written in form, respectively in clauses 4.2 and 4.3. The procedure of the latter is important. The architect should

issue instructions in writing in the first place, but it often occurs
that some oral matter is given on site or by telephone. If so either
the architect or the contractor may do the confirming and there
is a tight timetable for this. Presumably the architect will write
what he means if he does the confirming, while the contractor may
misinterpret him if he confirms. There is therefore a waiting period
in the latter instance for the architect to disagree. Only when the
instruction is properly constituted, need it be obeyed. The architect must be alive to urgent issues and ensure that he puts them
in writing promptly.

Not infrequently, matters miss this network of confirmation but
are still acted upon. The backstop provision therefore is for the
architect to confirm the instruction at any later time and for the
effect to be retrospective to the original date, a precise time which
may be important in some cases.

A number of clauses bear on the question of the architect's right
to check that the works are being produced in accordance with the
contract, to meet the contractor's obligation under clause 2.1. The
architect's duty to the employer to do this under his own contract
of engagement is beyond the present discussion, although it does
limit the architect's responsibility. What the present clauses do is
to give the architect facilities during progress, so that he does not
have to wait and simply check the completed works as best he can.
On the other hand these clauses do not oblige him to carry out
any checks on the way through, nor do they require him to express
any approval. His actions may be accompanied by silence or
disapproval if he wishes, and strictly he may defer any condemnation until after the works are complete. His only contractual
approval is contained in the final certificate under clause 30.8. In
practice, various degrees of consensus are reached during
progress, but these should never be expressed as final and if
necessary should be qualified as interim, so as not to conflict with
clause 30.10.

Only the 'reasonable satisfaction' provision of clause 2.1 needs
further comment here. If the contractor fails in any other respect
to comply with clause 2.1 then, as has been indicated, he is in
breach whether the architect notices the fault or not. But when
something is to be to the architect's reasonable satisfaction, *he* is
liable to check that it is so and, if he misses it, for the consequences
perhaps long after the works are complete, as is discussed under
clause 30.8. The architect therefore has a strong incentive to check
in these cases, or so to specify as not to use the term!

The power to check on materials and workmanship is conferred
by clause 8. Such vouchers as delivery notes and test certificates
may be obtained under clause 8.2. More importantly to cover

workmanship not only direct inspection, but also opening up and testing may be required under clause 8.3, either before or after fixing. In principle there is no limit to this and the architect may regularly have work torn apart, repeatedly if he wishes, or may wait until a late stage before having early work tested. Further he may choose 'any test'. In practice his instructions are moderated by the purpose of showing whether materials and workmanship are 'in accordance with this Contract', so that if he seeks to prove too much he is raising the specification and leading by implication to an extra variation payment. Even more compelling, liability between employer and contractor for the cost of all the inspection etc. and the consequent disturbance and making good is determined by whether or not there was a defect. The alternative to undefined testing is testing which is defined in nature and occurrence, such as specific routine testing of concrete cubes. If this is required, the prices in the contract bills usually include for the cost and no extra will then be payable.

The follow-up from this under clause 8.4 is for the architect to instruct the removal of defective materials and work. The clause does not mention that this removal and replacement are to be without extra charge, as this is implied by the contractor's obligation under clause 2.1 to complete the works in accordance with the contract.

Clause 8.5 is also a follow-on by allowing the architect to instruct the exclusion from the works of any employee. It may be inferred that this is to eliminate any persistent bad performer, as the contractor will usually himself seek to do.

To make inspection practicable the architect must be able to enter the site and workshops off-site, a right that he does not have automatically. Clause 11 provides for this and includes the architect's 'representatives' on the one hand and sub-contractors' workshops on the other. This covers the clerk of works under the next clause and can be stretched to cover the quantity surveyor as well. The right of access does not extend to suppliers, as this would be intolerably wide and impracticable for mass-produced goods.

To make inspection sufficiently detailed, clause 12 allows the employer to appoint a clerk of works who is controlled by the architect for day-to-day purposes, whoever actually employs him. The only formal duty of this person is to inspect and, by inference, to report his findings to the architect. He has no power to give instructions, even as a mouthpiece of the architect, including even those leading to a variation and to the removal of defective materials and work. (In passing, even less than the architect can he approve anything). In practice the clerk of works is a very useful member of the team to both architect and contractor in various of these ways. The clause therefore recognises that he may give 'directions' (not 'instructions'), but then makes these 'of no effect' unless confirmed by the architect and thus adopted as instructions. Only '2 working days' are allowed for confirmation so that if there is delay, a most likely thing, strictly the architect must reissue the directions as his own instructions. There is no provision for the contractor to confirm back either oral or written directions to either the clerk of works or the architect to give them any effect. Until these become instructions the contractor may ignore them. The procedure is not conducive to effective working and calls for a greater measure of clearly defined delegation in practice.

Another quite critical action of the architect is the issue of certificates, which clause 5.8 provides go to the employer with a copy to the contractor. The various general effects of certificates have been covered in Chapter 1 and these are true here, as may be seen from the certificates issuable under various clauses and summarised under 'Architect' in Chapter 13. In the case of certificates the architect is standing between the parties to the contract to exercise a function, rather than passing requirements to the contractor for the employer's benefit, as he is with instructions. Although he is not acting as an arbitrator, he has to decide evenly between them. If either party is dissatisfied over a certificate, he has the option to go to arbitration against the other party (not the architect) to seek redress.

Financial matters
The major element here is the contract sum. This is the 'lump sum' on which this entire contract is based financially. It in turn is based on the tendered figures which, with any agreed tidying up of errors before acceptance, are embodied in the contract bills. The question of error in the contract bills has been taken up under 'Documents and information' in this chapter. Clause 14.2 makes explicit the fixed nature of the contract sum, subject only to adjusting the permitted errors and to those other adjustments permitted in the conditions, which are discussed in various chapters and listed under 'Contract sum' in Chapter 15.

Clause 3 gives authority for adjustment to be taken into account in interim certificates for payment when they have been 'ascertained in whole or in part'. This expression may be read as referring to 'the whole approximately ascertained' or to 'a part precisely (or even approximately) ascertained' to permit inclusion as soon as possible. Some amounts are subject to retention, whereas others are allowable gross.

The matters of fees and charges under clause 6.2 have been discussed as part of 'Contractor's actions'. There remain royalties and patent rights under clause 9, which have a primarily financial impact. Clause 9.1 deals with work included in the contract sum and clause 9.2 with work arising from an architect's instruction. The former provides that the relevant royalties etc. are included in the contract sum and so are damages, etc. for infringement of patent, while the latter provides that both are to be added to the contract sum. Where extra work is of a type already included in the contract, this addition will be automatic by virtue of using the contract prices, otherwise it must be assessed. In the case of damages etc. the addition does seem unfair to the employer if the contractor has acted rashly.

CHAPTER 4

OTHER PERSONS WORKING ON THE SITE

GENERAL CONSIDERATIONS

Most of the clauses of the JCT conditions may be read as expressing and strengthening the otherwise implied terms of a building contract given in Chapter 1. These include the contractor's duty and right to perform the whole of the works in a workmanlike way to an adequate standard and in a reasonable time, and also his right to possession of the site for this purpose. While this is so, the conditions do introduce modifications in a number of ways, of which the question of persons other than the contractor performing some part of the works or some other contemporary work on site is one of the most important. These modifications are achieved by the clauses considered in varying detail in this chapter and in two cases enlarged upon in the next, while some of their effects are dealt with by subsidiary provisions in other clauses primarily about other matters, such as the programme, loss and expense and fluctuations.

The situations with which the clauses deal may be grouped into three categories:

(a) The contractor may wish to hand out to other persons the performance of work under the contract, even though he will still remain liable for the work, as is mentioned in Chapter 1. This is the subject of clause 19 and may take one of two forms: assignment in which the contractor hands out performance of the complete works, and sub-letting in which he hands out some defined parcel of work. In the latter case the contractor has a wide option to sub-let under the general law and the clause is restricting this. It appears to be concerned only with work performed at least partly on site and defines the person performing it as a domestic sub-contractor. (The clause also deals with assignment by the employer, which is therefore referred to in this chapter for completeness.)

(b) The employer or the architect on his behalf may oblige the contractor to have other persons of their choice performing work. This may take several forms. Firstly, the architect may nominate persons to the contractor whom he has to accept to perform defined parcels of work on or off-site. When they work at least partly on site they are defined as nominated sub-contractors and are the subject of clause 35. When they simply supply materials or goods to the site they are defined as nominated suppliers and dealt with by clause 36. Secondly, the employer may perform work on site alongside or even within the works or have it performed by persons who are under direct contract with him and who have no contractual relationship with the contractor. These cases are covered in clause 29 and the work is divided into two types: that about which the contractor was given warning in the contract bills in sufficient detail to be able to include in his tender for its effects, and that about which the detail was insufficient or which was not mentioned at all. (In passing, clauses 25 and 26 mention also the case of the employer or others on his behalf supplying materials to the contractor for use in the works, but clause 29 does not cover this aspect.)

(c) Both the employer and the contractor may be obliged to have a public body performing work under its statutory duties. Even if this constitutes part of the work so that it is paid for through the contractor, it is defined by clause 6.3 as not sub-contractor's work, although its status is not then positively defined. In particular, the provisions about nominated sub-contractors cannot be applied and no alternative is given, so that matters are left unhelpfully vague. It may otherwise not be part of the works and so fall within clause 29.

It is the pattern of the contract that none of these categories of work nor the other category of work which the contractor carries out himself shall be transmuted into one of the others without the consent of the contractor. Thus the contractor either himself decides to sub-let particular work or he is given prior warning in the contract bills that he must do so. He cannot otherwise be instructed to do so. Similarly, he cannot be given a variation instruction turning some of his work into the same work but done by a nominated firm, or an instruction doing the reverse, cases mentioned under clauses 13.1.3 and 35.2. Again, work of any of these cannot be omitted from the contract to be performed concurrently by another. How far fresh work can be added into the contract without variation of the contract occurring (see Chs 1 and 9) is a more difficult matter to define. It is of course open to the parties to arrange any of these exchanges mutually and upon suitable terms to take up the result. There is also the incidental ebb and flow of work between the various categories in the contract, as variations produce marginal changes in the physical work.

There are however several issues arising, not between the

categories, but in their individual operating procedures. The more important concern how to control or approve what the other party wants, with safeguards to both parties. The solutions adopted arise under the clauses, but may also be summarised here:

(a) Assignment by either party is unconditionally dependent upon the consent of the other.

(b) Sub-letting by the contractor to one of several named persons may be required by the architect through the contract bills. If proposed by the contractor, it is subject to the architect's 'reasonable consent'.

(c) Nomination by the architect is dependent upon identification of the work in the contract bills and upon particular terms being included in the sub-contract with the person proposed. In the case of a nominated sub-contractor the contractor also has a right of 'reasonable objection' to the person as such.

(d) The introduction of other persons working directly for the employer, or even of the employer carrying out work himself, creates no extra contractual relationship over the work itself with the contractor. It is however subject, as already mentioned, to the contractor being given information in the contract bills or otherwise having the right to withhold consent if the work would seriously disrupt his own.

These solutions all deal with the mechanics, but they are related to the reasons for using these approaches, most of which have a connection with specialisation. Prominent among them are concern over quality of work, meeting the programme, statutory necessity, paying an economical price and obtaining a design service. They may affect either party in varying measure, although the contractor has no design responsibility except over his own temporary works. How the employer benefits over design is discussed in the next chapter. In the cases of assignment and sub-letting, there is no change in the money passing between the parties themselves, whatever happens in the related arrangement. In the case of nomination, the employer usually faces an adjustment of the contract sum when the account of the nominated person is substituted for the prime cost sum, or possibly provisional sum, in the contract bills. This in turn removes from the contractor any unexpected financial consequence in this case.

The contractor stands between all the other parties, including the employer, in various respects. The clauses seek to leave him responsible for each type of supplier and sub-contractor. In the case of nominated persons some reduction of his responsibility occurs, especially over the programme, and at the same time some extra control of them by the architect is introduced. Linked with this are the provisions over loss and expense caused to the contractor by nominated persons and direct contractors of the employer. Only in the case of domestic sub-contractors is there no concession in the conditions.

There follows a synopsis of and comments on the clauses dealing with domestic sub-contractors and persons under direct contract. The clauses on nominated persons are taken in the next chapter with some reference to the related documents for sub-contractors and suppliers.

SYNOPSIS OF CLAUSES 19, 29

CLAUSE 19: ASSIGNMENT AND SUB-CONTRACTS
19.1 • Neither party may assign contract without consent of the other
19.2 • Contractor may not sub-let to domestic sub-contractor
    • without architect's consent
    • consent not to be unreasonably withheld
19.3 • Contract bills may contain list of possible domestic sub-contractors
    • for defined work, measured/described and priced by contractor
    • contractor must select one of list to perform work
  • List to be at least three persons
    • Employer/architect or contractor may add persons
    • subject to consent of other
  • If list drops to less than three persons
    • employer (not architect) or contractor may add to restore to three, or
    • contractor may perform, or
    • contractor may sub-let as clause 19.2
19.4 • Employment of domestic sub-contractor automatically determines with that of contractor
19.5 • Nominated sub-contractors covered elsewhere
    • Contractor not obliged to perform nominated sub-contract work

CLAUSE 29: WORKS BY EMPLOYER OR PERSONS EMPLOYED OR ENGAGED BY HIM
29.1 • If contract bills give adequate information for contractor's purposes on work
    • not part of contract
    • by employer of his direct contractors
  • Contractor to allow it

29.2 • If contract bills do not give information as above
  • on similar work
  • Contractor may allow it
    • consent not to be unreasonably withheld
29.3 • These persons
  • not sub-contractors
  • employer's responsibility regarding injury provisions

COMMENTS ON CLAUSES 19, 29

These two clauses legislate for diametrically distinct cases, as the introduction to this chapter has indicated: work for which the contractor is responsible and perhaps may perform himself, and that which he in no way performs and does not control, unless he does so in some respects by consultation through the employer.

Clause 19.1 is itself distinct from the rest of clause 19 and simply prohibits assignment by either party of his whole part in the contract without the consent of the other. Assignment is considered in principle in Chapter 1. The absence in the clause of 'reasonable' means that a party cannot be obliged to give consent and that arbitration over this is excluded.

Domestic sub-contractors
The more important topic in day-to-day terms is sub-contracting, here also termed sub-letting. In this clause the initiative is with the contractor and the term 'domestic sub-contractor' is used, as the sole alternative to 'nominated sub-contractor'. Any work which is not reserved as nominated may be a candidate for subletting. However under clause 19.2 the contractor must seek the architect's consent to a particular sub-letting, although here the inclusion of 'unreasonably' does help him greatly. The architect could withhold consent on grounds of the poor quality of the proposed sub-contractor's work or performance. The question of pricing does not arise, as the contractor is paid at the prices in the contract bills. The architect's decision is essentially related to quality. In turn the contractor cannot insist on a sub-contractor solely because his prices are so favourable, or even that they are the basis of the prices in the contract bills. In a critical case, the contractor should seek approval before his tender is accepted.

There may be classes of work which the architect requires to be undertaken by a specialist, but for which he does not seek the more complicated system of nomination. Clause 19.3 requires that there should be a list of permitted persons in the contract bills. The contractor will of course base his tender on prices from one of these persons and has 'sole discretion' as to whom he chooses, since the architect has done his approving in advance. The procedure for adding further names allows the contractor an option to propose persons on the clause 19.2 basis, and presumably these would be his favoured choice. It also allows the employer or the architect to expand the list subject to the consent of the contractor, who in any case could choose to ignore the persons added, except in so far as they avert the next stage. This is that the list is brought back up to three names by agreement of the employer with the contractor. But as an alternative to this and *not* as a next stage, the contractor may do the work himself without specific approval or may seek approval to sub-let under clause 19.2. This is complicated and untidy as a procedure, quite apart from the introduction of the employer and the partial exclusion of the architect in the detailed wording, and lends itself to possible abuse by either party.

The subsidiary provision about determination releases the sub-contractor so that he can enter into an arrangement with the employer or with a new contractor, although strictly it conflicts with the assignment arrangement in clause 27.4.1, as there will be nothing to assign.

The reference to nominated sub-contractors clarifies that the contractor cannot be forced to do any of their work.

There is a standard form of domestic sub-contract (published not by the JCT, but by the National Federation of Building Trades Employers) which is very similar to the standard forms of nominated sub-contracts at all appropriate points. It is not essential to the scheme of the contract to use this domestic form, in the way that it is to use one of the nominated forms. It certainly is helpful to do so for the larger sub-contract, although it is rather elaborate for small parcels of work.

Other persons
Clauses 29.1 and 29.2 refer to the same class of persons: the employer himself, his employees and his direct contractors, any of whom may be performing work which is not in the contract. The only distinction is whether the contractor receives adequate information in the contract bills. This information is to enable him to do his own work, but it also should allow him to include in the contract sum for any costs attributable to the interaction of his activities with the activities of these persons. If he has the information he must allow them on site. If he has not, then the employer has to seek his consent to them coming on site. This consent is not to be 'unreasonably withheld'. This allows account to be taken of potential disturbance of the contractor's activities

or of the need for special facilities and of whether an extra payment can be agreed to compensate for these under clause 26 or otherwise. In an extreme case there could be the possibility of frustration if such persons come on site, and the contractor could withhold consent quite reasonably.

If the contract bills provide some information but not enough, clause 29.2 will apply and so the contractor should be asked before signing the contract to confirm whether the information is enough to avoid later dispute. If the information is adequate but the work in question is then changed, clause 29.2 as worded does not come into play. Strictly, neither does the system of architect's instructions, whether as variations or otherwise. Unless something quite different in character is proposed, the parties are both committed and they must come to the best arrangement in the circumstances. In view of the complication inherent in clause 19.3, it is as well that the present clause does not try to provide an answer in what could be a variety of situations.

These persons are defined by clause 29.3 as those 'for whom the Employer is responsible' in terms of the indemnities over injury in clause 20.1. They are not sub-contractors and so again are completely distinct from domestic sub-contractors and nominated sub-contractors. Because what they produce is not part of the works, liability for damage to it will not fall to the contractor under clause 20.2 unless he is negligent or otherwise in default.

CHAPTER 5

NOMINATION OF SUB-CONTRACTORS AND SUPPLIERS

GENERAL CONSIDERATIONS OVER SUB-CONTRACTORS

Brief reference is made under 'General considerations' in Chapter 4 to nominated sub-contractors and suppliers, to compare them with domestic sub-contractors and those directly engaged by the employer. This chapter deals with both types of nominated persons more fully, although the remarks immediately following refer only to nominated sub-contractors at most points. The provisions regarding them are more elaborate than those for nominated suppliers, so that the exact position of the latter may be reserved until clause 36 is discussed.

Nomination principles

The system of nomination is largely peculiar to the construction industry. On the one hand it allows the architect to select a particular person to perform work, when that person is suitable as a specialist in one or more ways, such as quality of work, performance and organisation, price level and providing the architect with the whole design or developing parts of it for him. On the other hand when the architect nominates the selected person to the contractor, it is so that the contractor may first consider any peculiar aspects in the case and, in the light of these and of an otherwise known contractual framework, then enter into his own sub-contract with that person. Thereafter the person is in the same legal relationship to the contractor as is a domestic sub-contractor, and in particular must receive all instructions etc. from the architect through the contractor. The relationship is subject to a few special elements embodied in the conditions, both in the clauses immediately considered and elsewhere (see Ch. 13).

There are two presumed reasons for these special elements. One is to relieve somewhat the responsibilities of the contractor for lapses in programme by such a sub-contractor, as some compensation for having to accept a person not of his own choice. As a result, the employer is disadvantaged and has no immediate redress against the sub-contractor, because he has no direct contractual relationship with him. The other reason is to give the sub-contractor some protection, at least at the employer's discretion, against lapses by the contractor in paying him so that the employer pays the sub-contractor direct and recovers from the contractor, again reflecting the rather special status of the sub-contractor. This again is itself a commercial disadvantage to the employer, as he incurs an additional liability.

Nomination methods and sub-contract documents
As well as clause 35 of the main contract, there are several independent documents relating to nominated sub-contractors. There are also two methods of nomination, both covered in clause 35, but each relating to distinct sets of these independent documents. These methods are known, outside the contract, as the 'basic' and 'alternative' methods. The basic method is the more rigorously defined and is intended for sub-contracts which are the larger or more complex, although no criteria are made explicit. It requires the following mandatory separate documents, as well as clause 35 of the contract:

Sub-Contract Tender and Agreement	NSC/1
Employer/Nominated Sub-Contractor Agreement	NSC/2
Sub-Contractor Nomination	NSC/3
Nominated Sub-Contract	NSC/4

Of these documents, the first two receive some comment below, before dealing with the parts of clause 35 relevant to the theme of this chapter. Of the others, while nomination is a simple one-page instruction, the sub-contract is a document on the same scale as the main contract and very similarly worded in equivalent clauses, although its clauses are partly in a different order for no apparent reason. It is not commented upon separately, but some of its provisions are outlined in discussing clause 35 and other parts of the main contract in appropriate chapters.

With the alternative method, there are only two prescribed documents and of these the former is optional:

Employer/Nominated Sub-Contractor Agreement	NSC/2a
Nominated Sub-Contract	NSC/4a

Both these documents are very similar to their basic method counterparts. The virtues of using the agreement to protect the employer and the contractor in all but the most trivial cases need no further emphasis. It is necessary to supply counterparts to the tender and the nomination for the alternative method, the tender being open to more variation in its complexity. Under both methods, the tender includes the various documents such as drawings and is itself referred to in and incorporated into the sub-contract.

Nomination procedures

Each of the documents listed above is referred to in clause 35 of the main contract, which requires the intended method for each sub-contract to be identified in the contract bills. The parts of the nomination procedure following receipt of a desirable sub-contract tender and up to the nomination instruction may be discerned in the clause. The main elements of the larger process of selecting and nominating a sub-contractor and dealing with him thereafter with relevant parts, if any, of clause 35 are as follows:

(a) Selecting one or more potential sub-contractors for the parcel of work on relevant criteria (clause 35.2).

(b) Obtaining a tender that isolates one person as the most desirable (clauses 35.2 and 35.5).

(c) Setting up a collateral agreement between the employer and the sub-contractor, unless this is not required under the alternative method (clauses 35.6, 35.11, 35.20 and 35.21).

(d) Obtaining or setting in motion and then approving any design or specification work by the sub-contractor (no clause reference).

(e) Introducing the contractor and the proposed sub-contractor, so that they may agree any commercial, technical or operational points about the work that affect them both (clauses 35.7 and 35.10.1).

(f) Allowing for objections at this stage from the contractor or sub-contractor to be resolved, or for another sub-contractor to be found (clauses 35.4, 35.8, 35.9 and 35.23).

(g) Nominating the sub-contractor, so that he and the contractor enter into a binding contract (clauses 35.10.2, 35.11.2 and 35.12).

(h) Issuing information and instructions, inspecting and approving the sub-contractor's work and generally acting in the same ways over the physical work as towards the contractor, but acting in all matters through the contractor (no clause reference).

(i) Agreeing and certifying interim payments to the sub-contractor through the contractor, but operating safeguards for the sub-contractor (clause 35.13, and also clauses 30.2–30.6).

(j) Agreeing and certifying final payments to the sub-contractor as last (clause 35.17, and also clause 30.8).

(k) Instructing contractor on what extensions of time may be granted to the sub-contractor (clauses 35.14 and 35.15, also clause 25).

(l) Exercising some control over threatening determination of the sub-contractor's employment by the contractor and, if determination occurs in any way (including if the sub-contractor himself determines), nominating another sub-contractor (clauses 35.24 and 35.25).

(*m*) Seeing that any residual liabilities of the sub-contractor affecting the employer are settled through the contractor (clauses 35.16, 35.18, 35.19 and 35.22).

Subsidiary sub-contract documents
Tender NSC/1 for use with the basic method consists of four parts and it is to be expected that the tender under the alternative method would contain much of this at whatever level of detail was suitable:

(*a*) The tender and agreement proper: this contains general information about the sub-contract works and references to the other sub-contract documents. The sub-contract itself refers to and incorporates the tender as part of the sub-contract, in a way that the main contract does not provide for its tender, so that all the documents are united here. The sub-contract sum or other basis and the provision for 2½% cash discount for prompt payment for the contractor also occur here. There is no reference to any design or specification by the sub-contractor.

(*b*) Stipulations: these relate to withdrawal of the tender while it is under consideration and cognate matters.

(*c*) Particulars of main contract and sub-contract: these are to be given by the architect when the tender is invited and are to be supplemented by details of site conditions, etc.

(*d*) Particular conditions: these are relative details not in conflict in the foregoing and to be agreed between the contractor the sub-contractor before final nomination, such as points of attendance to be provided.

Agreement NSC/2, obligatory with the basic method, and Agreement NSC/2a, optional with the alternative method, are almost identical and are used to overcome the problem of no privity of contract between the employer and the sub-contractor and to create a limited arrangement collateral to the main contract and the sub-contract. Under these agreements, the sub-contractor indemnifies the employer against the losses which he may suffer by virtue of the main contract provision over extension of time which relieves the contractor and shields the sub-contractor. He also indemnifies the employer against any loss caused by a determination of the sub-contract due to his own default. This agreement of the sub-contractor is in consideration of being nominated and of an otherwise optional provision for direct payment on the contractor's default becoming obligatory. Such payment is a power granted under main clause 35 that would not otherwise be available to the employer. It might of course be questioned whether it would be less complex simply to delete the special elements in the contract and then not to use the collateral agreement.

There are though two other important provisions in the agreement, not strictly related to those already mentioned. The one imposes on the sub-contractor a liability towards the employer over any design work that the sub-contractor may perform under the sub-contract. This is important because the contractor has no design responsibility under the contract with the employer, so that without the agreement there would be no means of redress for the employer. As a side effect, this also protects the architect who has quite properly sub-let part of his design commitment to the sub-contractor in the specialist area concerned. The provision relates both to delay in performing design and to faults in the design. The other provision allows the employer to have design and fabrication work done by the sub-contractor ahead of nomination and to pay for it direct, whether the nomination goes ahead or not. This may save programme time in some cases. Neither the main contract nor the sub-contract refers in any way to either design or early fabrication, or to the question of direct payment.

SYNOPSIS OF CLAUSE 35

The whole clause is given here for completeness, although clauses 35.13–35.19 are commented upon in the chapters dealing more widely with their subject-matter in the contract.

GENERAL

35.1 • Definition of nominated sub-contractor to contractor
  • where architect has reserved selection and approval by
    • prime cost sum, or
    • naming sub-contractor
  • in/by
    • contract bills, or
    • instruction expending provisional sum, or
    • instruction of variation, only if work
      • extra to contract *and*
      • similar to other nominated work, or
    • agreement (not unreasonably withheld) between contractor and architect
  • This applies notwithstanding definition in SMM6
35.2 • Contractor may tender for nominated sub-contract work in contract bills, provided
  • he ordinarily does such work himself

- item given in appendix
- architect prepared to receive tender
- This without prejudice to right to reject tender
- If contractor's tender accepted, not to sub-let without consent
- May be extended to work arising out of provisional sum
- Clauses to apply
  - clause 13 variations
  - clause 35.2, but not rest of clause' 35
35.3 • List of documents for nominated sub-contractors
  - tender NSC/1
  - agreements NSC/2 and NSC/2a
  - nomination NSC/3
  - sub-contract NSC/4 and NSC/4a

NOMINATION PROCEDURE

35.4 • No one to be nominated if contractor has reasonable objection
  - This to be as soon as possible
    - with basic method, not later than sending NSC/1 to architect
    - with alternative method, not later than 7 days after nomination instruction
35.5 • Basic method to be used unless alternative method expressly included
  - with this, NSC/1 and NSC/2 necessary
  - Alternative method to be used
    - if contract bills, nomination instruction or expending provisional sum so state
    - to be stated whether NSC/2a to be used
  - Whichever method is stated
    - may be changed by variation
    - not later than
      - preliminary nomination, basic method
      - nomination instruction, alternative method

BASIC METHOD

35.6 • This method to be used, unless alternative method used
35.7 • Architect's action prior to nomination
  - arrange for proposed sub-contractor to
    - tender on NSC/1
    - complete NSC/2
  - send to contractor
    - NSC/1
    - copy NSC/2

- preliminary nomination and instruction to settle particular conditions
- Contractor to proceed to settle

35.8
- Contractor to inform architect within 10 working days
  - if unable to agree, giving reasons
  - but to keep trying
- Architect to instruct as necessary

35.9
- Contractor to inform architect immediately
  - if sub-contractor withdraws offer
  - and stop action
- Architect to instruct further

35.10
- Contractor to send architect
  - completed NSC/1, with particular conditions
  - as soon as settled
- Architect to nominate sub-contractor forthwith, on NSC/3

ALTERNATIVE METHOD

35.11
- Employer to conclude NSC/2a with proposed sub-contractor, if required
- Architect to nominate sub-contractor, with instruction

35.12
- Contractor to conclude NSC/4a within 14 days

PAYMENT OF SUB-CONTRACTOR

35.13
- Architect at each interim certificate, for each sub-contractor to
  - direct contractor on amount
    - of interim/final payment included
    - as NSC/4 or NSC/4a
  - inform sub-contractor of amount
- Contractor to make interim payments as NSC/4 or NSC/4a
- Contractor to provide architect with proof of discharge before next interim certificate
- Architect may take no action if
  - contractor fails to provide proof, and
  - architect satisfied sole reason is lapse by sub-contractor over evidence
- If unjustified lack of proof
  - employer
    - may operate direct payment procedure
    - must do so if NSC/2 or NSC/2a apply
  - architect to certify
    - lack of proof and amount
    - with copy to sub-contractor

- employer may/must
  - reduce future payments to contractor by amount, plus any VAT
  - pay amount to sub-contractor
  - provided employer not paying out more than in hand
- employer's action subject to
  - paying sub-contractor
    - at same time as contractor paid any balance, or
    - within 14 days of due date, if no balance for contractor
  - if retention only due to contractor, not deducting other than contractor's own retention
  - when several sub-contractors to pay and total available inadequate
    - apportion pro rata, or
    - use other fair and reasonable method
  - *no* action to be taken if contractor being wound up

EXTENSION OF PERIOD(S)

35.14
- Contractor not to give sub-contractor any extension, except
  - in accordance with NSC/4 or NSC/4a
  - with architect's consent
- Architect to operate NSC/4 or NSC/4a, after
  - notice, particulars and estimate, and request for extension
  - all from contractor and sub-contractor

FAILURE TO COMPLETE

35.15
- Architect to
  - certify to contractor failure of sub-contractor to complete
  - send copy to sub-contractor within 2 months of notice
- Provided
  - contractor notified architect
  - contractor sent copy to sub-contractor

PRACTICAL COMPLETION

35.16
- Architect to certify practical completion of sub-contract
  - for purposes of this clause and final payment
  - to send copy to sub-contractor

FINAL PAYMENT OF SUB-CONTRACTOR

35.17
- Architect to issue interim certificate to include final

payment to sub-contractor
- any time after practical completion, with maximum of 12 months
- provided
  - NSC/2 or NSC/2a in force
  - clause 5 or clause 4 respectively thereof in force unamended
- and provided sub-contractor
  - remedied defects, to satisfaction of architect and contractor
  - sent all necessary final account documents through contractor to architect/quantity surveyor

35.18
- Architect to nominate substituted sub-contractor to remedy defects,
  - as full nominated sub-contractor under this clause
  - if sub-contractor fails to remedy defects, after final payment and before final certificate
- Employer to try to recover substituted price
  - from original sub-contractor
  - under NSC/2 or NSC/2a
- Contractor to pay or allow employer
  - any deficiency in recovery
  - provided he agreed to substituted price
- This clause not to override clause 35.21

35.19
- Notwithstanding final payment of sub-contractor
  - contractor responsible until practical completion or possession
    - for loss or damage to such work
    - to same extent as rest of works
  - applicable version of clause 22 still in force

POSITION OF EMPLOYER

35.20
- Employer's liability to sub-contractor
  - not by virtue of powers in clause 35
    - even if used
  - only by virtue of NSC/2 or NSC/2a

POSITION OF CONTRACTOR

35.21
- Contractor's liability to employer
  - not by NSC/2 or NSC/2a
  - but still fully by virtue of this contract

RESTRICTIONS IN CONTRACTS OF SALE

35.22
- Liability of contractor to employer limited
  - to same extent as that of sub-contractor to contractor

POSITION WHEN NOMINATION DOES NOT PROCEED
35.23 • Architect to
        • omit proposed work, or
        • select another person for nomination
    • If
        • contractor reasonably objects
        • proposed sub-contractor does not within reasonable time
            • settle particular conditions, if under NSC/1, or
            • enter into NSC/4a, if applicable

RENOMINATION
35.24 • If one of three situations arises
        • contractor informs that sub-contractor is in default under NSC/4 or NSC/4a, and
            • contractor passed sub-contractor's observations to architect
            • architect agrees with contractor
        • sub-contractor insolvent
        • sub-contractor determines own employment under NSC/4 or NSC/4a
    • Then
        • in the first situation
            • architect to give instruction to contractor
                • to give notice of default to sub-contractor
                • possibly requiring contractor to obtain further instruction before determination
            • contractor to inform architect
                • whether determined after first instruction
                • that determined after (any) second instruction
            • architect to make further nomination of sub-contractor to complete
                • after such determination
                • providing contractor has opportunity to agree to substituted price
                    • if determination due to default over defects
        • in the second situation
            • architect to make further nomination of sub-contractor to complete
            • but architect may delay doing so
                • if reinstatement likely
                • without prejudice to interests of any involved or to be involved
        • in the third situation
            • architect to make further nomination of sub-

contractor to complete
- but extra amount to be deducted from sums due to
- contractor
- Amounts payable to sub-contractors further nominated
  in first two situations to be included in payments

DETERMINATION OF SUB-CONTRACT
35.25 • Contractor not to determine sub-contract
- by any right acquired
- without architect's instruction
35.26 • When sub-contractor's employment determined for his
default
- architect to direct over amount for sub-contractor
  included in interim certificate
- this to be in accordance with NSC/4 or NSC/4a

COMMENTS ON CLAUSES 35.1–35.12, 35.20–35.26

These two sections of clause 35 are concerned with definitions,
stipulations and procedures most of which apply before the
appointment of a nominated sub-contractor and all of which are
related to each other more closely than they are to the intervening
section of the clause. The parts of that section are taken in other
chapters dealing with such matters as extension of time and
payments in general, while the sections taken here are not treated
entirely in the order of the clause.

General matters
Clause 35.1 establishes two related elements: that the nominated
person becomes a sub-contractor of the contractor, but that the
architect selects and approves him in the first place. Between these
two, there is the right of the contractor under clause 35.4 to object
to the person put forward by the architect. This objection must be
reasonable and this usually means objection to the known unsat-
isfactory performance of the person. 'Reasonable' signals the
possibility of arbitration and this clearly cannot be held over until
practical completion, even though it is not given as a matter for
immediate arbitration under article 5. Any objection should be
prompt and must be within the appropriate limit set in clause 35.4.
There is not a right of objection to the terms offered; these are
quite tightly constrained by the tender documentation and, under
the basic method, by the procedures prior to firm nomination.
Anything not expected from what is in the contract bills can be
dealt with by a variation instruction.

There are two ways given in clause 35.1 of identifying and reserving work for a nominated sub-contractor: by using a prime cost sum and by naming the sub-contractor. The clause also gives four situations in which either of these two may occur, on a strict reading of the clause. In practice the prime cost sum can logically be used alone only in the contract bills and naming in the other three situations, since the two ways would be meaningless if transposed among the four situations. It is possible to use a prime cost sum *and* naming in the contract bills, if a sub-contractor is known in advance, and this does give the contractor as much information as possible when he is tendering.

The first case of an inclusion in the contract bills and the last one of an agreement between the parties need little comment. The prime cost sum is omitted in the final account and the actual amount substituted in accordance with clause 30.6.2. When there is a special agreement, but only so, there may be any change of work from the contractor himself to a nominated person or the introduction of additional work of any type for a nominated person to perform. In any case, adjustment to some contract terms to suit such an agreement may, by inference, be part of the agreement.

The second case of work instructed as part of the expenditure of a provisional sum is not qualified as the others are. It appears, therefore, that the architect may nominate in respect of work of similar type to what is already measured and priced in the contract bills. This is inconsistent with clause 13.1.3 over variations, but not precisely in conflict with it, as the two sets of work are mutually exclusive. It is also inconsistent in policy with the third case of a nomination arising out of a variation. Here there is a limitation to work additional to what is shown in the contract, while also it must be work of a kind similar to that already set aside in the contract bills for a nominated sub-contractor.

Clause 35.2 is apart from the rest of the clause 35, as its last part indicates. It allows for the contractor tendering for nominated work, provided that he can meet all three conditions in clause 35.2.1. To have his intention included in the appendix, he must notify it before the contract is formalised, except when the work arises from a provisional sum. However, the most important factor is whether the architect is prepared to receive and the employer to accept a tender. Presumably if it is good commercial sense they will, despite the other stipulations. The contractor should be required to tender on a basis strictly comparable with any other persons, that is for his tender to include the equivalent of cash discount and with it understood that profit and attendances will be allowed over and above his tender. Alternatively, it should be made plain if any of these is not the case. Once the contractor is given the work he may not sub-let it; this time without the architect meeting the test of reasonableness, since it is intended to be work for the contractor to perform himself. The general variations provisions are drawn in: they may not fit precisely if there are no quantities in the tender.

Clause 35.3 simply gives the full titles of documents referred to in later parts of clause 35.

Clauses 35.20 and 35.21 make clarifying stipulations concerning the relationships of the employer, the contractor and the sub-contractor, which are both hierarchical and collateral. The clauses are opposite sides of the same coin. In the former clause it is confirmed that the employer's only liability to the sub-contractor is via Agreement NSC/2 or NSC/2a. For instance, the power to pay the sub-contractor direct under the contract exists in relation to the contractor, but the relationship with the sub-contractor over this exists because of the agreement. In the latter clause it is confirmed that the sub-contractor's responsibility towards the employer under clauses of the agreements does not extend the contractor's contractual liability. These clauses refer to 'design, materials, performance specification' over which the contractor has no responsibility for execution or choice and on which the contract is therefore silent. There are other matters in the agreements, over delay and disturbance for instance, but the contract is explicit on these.

Clause 35.22 relieves the contractor of a liability to the employer. Under the sub-contract, the sub-contractor may have to enter into a sub-sub-contract or a contract of sale containing restrictions of liability. This may be done with the consent of both the contractor and the architect and is particularly likely with standard, mass-produced articles. The sub-contractor is then relieved to that extent by the sub-contract and so clause 35.22 carries this relief into the main contract.

Nomination procedures
Clause 35.4 introduces the procedural clauses on nomination and has already been covered. Clause 35.5 treats both the basic and the alternative methods. The pattern is that the basic method applies, unless the alternative method is specially introduced for a particular sub-contract in one of the ways given. Whichever method is named, the architect may reverse matters, provided he does so before the appropriate stage. This is before all the detailed exchanges between contractor and sub-contractor under the basic method, but not until the last minute under the alternative method. In this second case, there will be then a regression to

allow the contractor to undertake the exchanges with the sub-contractor, which the alternative method has not prescribed and which need not have happened, and so some delay. As this change of method comes about by an instruction classed as a variation, it is possible to make any adjustment to the contract sum that may result. It may also modify the sub-contractor's tender but this is outside the present discussion. Agreement NSC/2 is obligatory under the basic method, whereas Agreement NSC/2a is optional under the alternative method. If therefore a sub-contractor is to tender under the alternative method, the contract bills or any instruction introducing a nomination must state whether or not Agreement NSC/2a is to be used. If a switch of nomination methods is considered, it is clearly easier to achieve if Agreement NSC/2a is intended to go with the alternative method, whether this method is being introduced or discarded. Otherwise the basis of the sub-contractor's tender will be disturbed and delay introduced. The relevant form of agreement is desirable anyway in any sub-contract of or above the significance likely to be switched.

The basic method procedure is introduced by clause 35.6, which again gives that method as the norm. It starts under clause 35.7.1 when a 'proposed sub-contractor has tendered', so that no preceding steps are given and any prior consultation with the contractor is quite informal. It also starts when the proposed sub-contractor has 'entered into Agreement NSC/2'. While the sub-contractor and probably the employer have now completed this document, it is so worded as not to become live until the architect signs the tender when also issuing the nomination instruction proper under clause 35.10.2 at the end of the procedure.

The straightforward order of events is that the architect sends the preliminary notice of nomination and other documents to the contractor; the contractor agrees any outstanding particular conditions of the tender (such as matters of attendance) with the proposed sub-contractor and returns the now completed tender to the architect. The tender will have been checked by the architect and probably the quantity surveyor earlier, is now satisfactory to the contractor and should still be so for the architect and the quantity surveyor, unless something untoward has been done. Nomination is a simple instruction and Agreement NSC/2 is activated. Oddly, the signing of the sub-contract is not mentioned (as it is for the alternative method), but is mandatory to complete the chain.

Clauses 35.8 and 35.9 deal with actions if affairs go slow or if there is deadlock between the contractor and sub-contractor over the particular conditions. The critical matters for the contractor will have been covered in the contract bills, if there was a prime cost sum, and for the sub-contractor in the tender, but there may be details over such things as attendance, siting of facilities and the programme to resolve. The contractor has ten working days before he must notify the architect that he has not finished, giving reasons. The architect has to issue instructions which may contain a concession to help relieve matters, but which may simply urge the contractor to continue negotiations. This in any case he should have been doing in the meantime. More critically, the sub-contractor may withdraw his offer and the contractor must then suspend activity until the architect gives further instructions. These again may lead to some concession to induce the sub-contractor back, or to action under clause 35.23 leading perhaps to a fresh nomination.

In any three-way activity of this nature, there is clearly the possibility of a number of options emerging. One likelihood is that of delay to the works by reason of a late nomination. This is not 'delay on the part of' a nominated sub-contractor, since one has not been nominated, but it is a delay over instructions that could lead to extension of time or payment for loss and expense. Whether it does will depend on the details of negotiations, so that there is room for dispute over liability.

The alternative method of procedure of clauses 35.11 and 35.12 omits most of these matters and, in particular, any preliminary notice of nomination and treating between the contractor and the proposed sub-contractor. There is a possibly longer period of fourteen days (but they are not 'working days') following the firm nomination, then ending in a sub-contract. There is no suggestion here of failure to agree, although clause 35.23 takes this up.

Clause 35.23 provides for two solutions if the contractor has a reasonable objection to a proposed sub-contractor or if negotiations come to a complete halt. The more likely is for the architect to put forward another proposed sub-contractor. The other is for him to omit the work, which in many cases will be physically inconceivable. The other solution not explicit in the clause is to offer revised terms, as already suggested, to start up discussions again with the originally proposed sub-contractor. These cases may intensify the question of delay.

Renomination procedures
A quite distinct question of delay arises if a nominated sub-contractor is lost by determination under his sub-contract, so that renomination becomes necessary. This is the theme of clause 35.24, which covers any timing of this event from the day after nomination until completion of the sub-contract work. There are three situations given in the first parts of the clause and three

corresponding sets of actions follow in the latter parts.

The first situation is that of default of the sub-contractor. The ways of default for the sub-contractor given in sub-contract clause 29.1 are the same as those given for the contractor himself in relation to the employer (considered in Ch. 7). Suspension of work by the sub-contractor must be read in the light of the special provision over non-payment in sub-contract clause 21.8, as suspension there is not a cause for determination under sub-contract clause 29.1. The instance of non-removal of defective work lacks the qualification about the works being materially affected, but is extended to cover failure to remedy defects etc. These may well come to light after completion of the sub-contract but while the contractor is still carrying out other parts of the works, and so may affect what he is doing. The contractor may not determine the sub-contractor's employment without carrying the architect with him. There is therefore the process of giving the architect information from both contractor and sub-contractor about the alleged default and of the architect confirming his agreement, if such it be, to the contractor and instructing him to issue a formal notice of default to the sub-contractor. This notice leads on to the contractor determining, but the architect may reserve the right to issue a further instruction before this happens. This allows the architect to see how serious affairs become in a borderline case, and thus whether determination and the resultant delay are justified. The contractor is to notify the architect when and if determination occurs.

Following on this situation, the architect is to make a further nomination to allow completion of the work. If remedial work is involved, the contractor is allowed to agree to the price of the sub-contractor on the same lines as in clause 35.18.1 (see Ch. 10). Clause 35.24.7 however provides for the *whole* of the substituted sub-contractor's account to be paid to the contractor, which is out of step with the other provision.

The second situation, that of insolvency, is an accomplished fact and leads directly to a further nomination, subject only to the architect holding back if reinstatement of the original sub-contractor is likely and is backed up by signs of revived efficiency. Again, clause 35.24.7 provides for the contractor to be paid the full amount of the substituted account.

The third situation is that of default by the contractor leading to the sub-contractor determining, but not at that time to a determination of the main contract by the employer. Here the sub-contractor may act without the architect's consent, so that again a further nomination is the only reasonable prospect. This is to be done without involving the contractor in agreement of the price, but any extra amount may be recovered by the employer directly from the contractor. This financial pattern does not assume that the contractor is necessarily in the wrong, only that he and the original sub-contractor will settle the question between them. Oddly though, clause 35.24.7 does not provide for the substituted amount to be paid to the contractor, as it should be.

In none of these situations, is detailed provision made here about settling with the original sub-contractor. In each case, the terms of the sub-contract will apply and so clause 35.25 provides that in no case must the contractor determine a sub-contract, as distinct from the sub-contractor's employment under it (see Ch. 7 on these terms), without an instruction from the architect. If he does, he may render himself liable to the employer and be unable to turn to the sub-contractor for recompense. Clause 35.26 provides for the first two situations, default and insolvency of the sub-contractor by reference to sub-contract clause 29.4. This gives a similar effect to that in a main contract determination under clause 27, but arranges the calculations differently. The architect has to direct over payments, and no more is due until after completion of the sub-contract work and finalisation of an account.

GENERAL CONSIDERATIONS OVER SUPPLIERS

Nomination of suppliers takes place for similar reasons to nomination of sub-contractors but, mainly because they do not perform work on site, the documentation about suppliers is less extensive and less complex. It consists of clause 36 of the contract and of a form of tender, which incorporates an optional warranty. The main simplications are:

(a) There is no defined nomination procedure: the form of tender requires a nomination by the architect and acceptance by the contractor. The contractor, by inference, may object to a nomination related to an inadequate contract of sale but not to a proposed person as such. There is no procedure for renomination, although a further nomination is straightforward to achieve.

(b) There are no stipulations about the contractor tendering for a nominated supply, about whether nomination or contractor's supply may be substituted in either direction or about the nominated supplier sub-letting manufacture.

(c) The contractor is to make payments as he judges them to be due: the architect does not direct payments through interim certificates and the contractor has to pay whether certificates include the amounts or not.

(*d*) The contractor may hold no retention, although the amounts are included in the total subject to contractor's retention as defined in clause 30.

(*e*) The supplier is not protected by the architect or the quantity surveyor checking that payments have been made, and the employer has no right or duty to make direct payments.

(*f*) The architect is not directly involved in settling questions of default over the programme of delivery as between the contractor and supplier, although such default may lead to the contractor securing an extension of time. The warranty is relevant here.

(*g*) There are no provisions about indemnity or insurance in respect of injury. The provisions about consequential expense due to defects are, however, more stringent than contracts of sale often give.

(*h*) Provisions about variations, fluctuations and a final account are limited and mainly rely on insertions in the tender.

(*i*) Reference to determination is restricted to determination of the contractor's own employment.

The form of tender is to contain or refer to the main particulars about quality and quantity, the overall programme and defects liability, as well as fluctuations rules as mentioned above. It repeats the contract of sale elements in clause 36.4, rather than restating them to read directly between the contractor and the supplier. They are in any case minimum terms and the use of the form of tender is not obligatory, so long as the terms are not overriden.

The warranty is a schedule in the form of tender, although the tender can be used without it. It has a collateral role, like that of the employer/nominated sub-contractor agreement. It contains provisions about the supplier's liability for design and specification in similar terms to those in the agreement. It says nothing about payment for work before nomination and, obviously from what has already been said, nothing about direct payments after nomination. The supplier does, however, give indemnities to the employer to protect him against expense or loss of a right to recovery caused by the supplier's default.

SYNOPSIS OF CLAUSE 36

CLAUSE 36: NOMINATED SUPPLIERS
36.1 • Definition of 'nominated supplier'
   • materials fixed by contractor
   • nominated by architect

- prime cost sum in contract bills, supplier named there or later
- by instruction expending provisional sum
  - supplier named, or
  - only one supplier possible
- by variation instruction
  - only one supplier possible
- Not to apply to materials
  - in contract bills with fixing by contractor
  - even if only one supplier possible
  - unless prime cost sum

36.2 • Architect to issue instruction to nominate supplier

36.3 • Amounts properly chargeable
  - total paid/payable to nominated supplier
  - including as applicable
    - tax or duty, other than VAT
    - packing and delivery, net of credits
    - any price adjustment
  - less all discounts, except permitted cash discount
- Extra expense of contractor to be added to contract sum

36.4 • Architect to nominate only person with contract of sale including
  - materials to be correct quality
  - making good defects, within defects liability period
    - including consequential expenses
    - providing examined before fixing
    - not due to mishandling etc.
  - delivery to be as agreed/reasonable programme
  - 5% cash discount allowed for full payment within 30 days of end of month
  - no deliveries after determination, unless paid for
  - contractor to pay within 30 days of end of month
  - ownership to pass to contractor on delivery, whether or not paid
  - joint arbitration provision, as article 5
  - no provision to override etc. any of this set

36.5 • Contractor's liability to employer for materials to be restricted etc.
  - to same extent as that of supplier to contractor
  - subject to
    - architect's approval
    - provisions following
- Contractor not obliged to enter contract with supplier
  - until architect approves restrictions etc.
- Nothing here to override clause 36.4

COMMENTS ON CLAUSE 36

Nomination and accounts

As in clause 35.1, so in clause 36.1 the two related elements are established that the nominated person has a contract with the contractor, but that the architect selects and approves him in the first place. The lack of defined procedures and of a right to object to the person have been noted, along with other omissions under 'General considerations' on this clause.

The first two ways in which a nomination may be made compare with those for a sub-contractor and relate to expending a sum in the contract bills. In the case of a prime cost sum the wording is more logical, as the naming cannot be read as an alternative to the sum. In the case of a provisional sum, the reference to a prime cost sum appears superfluous as no sum actually exists at any stage. It is presumably intended to ensure that the appropriate adjustments will be made in the final account.

The last two ways also contain a similar reference to a prime cost sum. More importantly, they have in common the criterion of a nomination arising when only one possible supplier of the materials exists, even though the architect does not name him or issue a nomination instruction. (There is a conflict here, as clause 36.1 uses the term 'deemed to have been nominated', while clause 36.2 requires the architect to issue an instruction.) In one case the architect instructs over expending a provisional sum and in the other he instructs a variation. Both therefore arise entirely post-contractually and the contract bills cannot have been priced to take account of sole source in any way. In the case of materials specified in the contract bills and having precisely the same supply limitation, clause 36.1.2 categorically defines them as *not* being subject to nominated supply so that no adjustment arises in the final account on that score. If further materials of this latter type are specified in expending a provisional sum or in a variation, they should be valued under clause 13 and not under the present arrangements, even though the present clause leaves the point open.

The tender will contain details of prices, but may or may not show a tender sum. Eventually the amounts 'properly chargeable to the Employer' under clause 36.3.1 are in any case to be arrived at by summation of all the appropriate accounts for the nominated supplier, whether paid at the time or not. These do not have to be agreed with the nominated supplier in all cases, as the contractor may be meeting extra accounts, for instance to cover replacements. Specifically they are to exclude such discounts as trade discounts and include just cash discount, larger on supply than on sub-contract payments. The tender should be checked before acceptance to take out inadmissible discounts and to clarify their effect on competitiveness. Otherwise the amounts chargeable are to include any of the three listed items that arise.

The contract bills will usually contain fixing items for materials that allow for costs from unloading onwards. Clause 36.3.2 gives authority for the contractor to be reimbursed any costs of his own, such as transport costs, in excess of the standard provisions and not covered in any other way.

Contract of sale

Clause 36.4 is concerned with the contract of sale and, as mentioned, its provisions are repeated in the tender. So too are clauses 36.3 and 36.5 which do not directly concern the supplier. The contractor and the supplier may agree any further terms, as 'inter alia' recognises, but these are to be taken in the light of the last of the nine terms given, so that any conflicting extra provision will be nullified. The other eight terms may be taken in order.

The first two terms relate to quality and defects respectively. Quality is defined in the same way as in clause 2.1: there is no reference to design and specification by the supplier and the tender warranty is important here. The supplier is responsible for remedying defects until the end of the defects liability period and also for such consequential expenses of the contractor as removing installed materials, refixing and making good other work disturbed. This is quite an extensive protection to the contractor, who is liable for all these costs under clause 17, but it is subject to the two provisos about inspection and care. After the defects liability period, the supplier will be subject to the wider law.

The third and fifth terms related to delivery. The programme may be incorporated in the contract of sale, but in any event is not a matter on which the architect can act. His only concern is over extension of time. The contractor has no special redress against the supplier, just the usual legal rights. If there is a main contract determination the supplier may suspend delivery, but not determine, although deliveries could be resumed after an assignment. The seventh term obviously makes it most advisable for the supplier to suspend deliveries.

Terms four and six are two sides of a coin, respectively requiring the supplier to allow cash discount for payment on time and requiring the contractor to make payment on time. They could have been written as one.

The eighth term relates to a joint arbitration, which is available if the appropriate parts of the article apply (see Ch. 15). Clause 36.5 is making a similar provision to that of clause 35.22 to protect the contractor. It goes further in its latter two stipulations to make explicit what might be held to be implicit.

CHAPTER 6

PROGRESS OF THE WORKS

GENERAL CONSIDERATIONS

The clauses taken in this chapter give the salient provisions over the progress of the works from the handing over of the site to the contractor to the handing back of the site with the completed works upon it to the employer and also extend into the period during which the contractor is responsible for the direct remedying of defects. The following general points may be noted:

(*a*) There is a defined contract construction period, with its beginning fixed and a latest date for its ending under clause 23. This, and a requirement for regular progress, cover what would otherwise be the implied, if less rigid terms (see Ch. 1).

(*b*) If the employer does not hand over the site on time, a possibility not mentioned in the conditions, he is liable for breach. If the contractor is late in completion, he is liable for liquidated damages (see Ch. 1) under clause 24. If he is dilatory in between he may lose his right to an extension of time (see (*c*)) and, in an extreme case, may be in danger of determination of his employment under clause 27.

(*c*) To protect the contractor, a number of events are given in clause 25 that entitle the contractor to be granted an extension of the completion date by a defined procedure. If this happens, the liability for liquidated damages is reduced to the extent that the completion date has been moved on. The extension procedure also protects the employer against the possibility of losing a closely controlled completion date, as is discussed under liquidated damages in Chapter 1.

(*d*) There is no provision entitling the employer to press for an acceleration of the programme in whole or in part, whether to achieve an earlier than contemplated completion or to make up lost time instead of granting an extension. This is so, even if the employer is willing to pay extra for such acceleration. Even when delay is entirely the fault of the contractor, all that can be done is to try to persuade him to amend his ways, backing this with the threat of liquidated damages if he is late or of determination if his dilatoriness becomes flagrant. There is however, rather ironically, a power for the architect to instruct a postponement of a part or even all of the works.

(e) Several of the grounds for extension of time have a relation to those for loss and expense in clause 26, but the right to either remedy does not necessarily entitle the contractor to the other. They are quite distinct provisions (see comparison table in Ch. 14).

(f) On practical completion of the works under clause 17, the contractor ceases to be liable to perform fresh work but is liable for a defined period to return and himself make good defects. During this period a monetary retention is held and beyond it the contractor still has liabilities for defects (see Ch. 1 about defective work and also clause 30).

(g) The preceding points all relate to a single completion date, even if this suffers delay. It is possible to have different completion dates for parts of the works, by one of two methods. Various dates may be written into the contract and the Sectional Completion Supplement (see Ch. 2) is then incorporated. Otherwise clause 18 allows for phased completion and handing over by agreement made during progress. These methods may both be used in one contract. They apportion such matters as liquidated damages, extension of time and defects liabilities.

(h) There is no provision for phased handing over of the site to the contractor, but it is reasonably straightforward to incorporate amendments into the conditions and the appendix to provide for this.

(i) The conditions say nothing about what is to happen if the contractor finishes very early, or even does a high proportion of work early in the programme, before perhaps the employer is able to raise funds for such rapid payment.

Subject to these points, the conditions are not specific about the contractor's order of working. He is required to provide and revise a master programme under the optional part of clause 5, but when this applies the programme is for information only and so the contractor may change his programme as he wishes. Only if there are stipulations in the contract bills on the order of working as allowed under clause 13 is the contractor constrained. The existence of such stipulations also gives the architect power to amend the order of working laid down, by way of reasonable variations. He can amend only what is laid down, so that if there are no stipulations he cannot instruct amendments at all.

SYNOPSIS OF CLAUSES 23–25

CLAUSE 23: DATE OF POSSESSION, COMPLETION AND POSTPONEMENT
23.1 • Employer has fixed date for giving contractor possession of site
     • Contractor has latest date for completing works
     • Between these dates
         • contractor to work steadily
23.2 • architect may instruct postponement of whole or part of works

CLAUSE 24: DAMAGES FOR NON-COMPLETION
24.1 • Architect to certify if contractor fails to complete by due date
24.2 • Employer may then
         • deduct liquidated damages from payments to contractor (who 'allows'), or
         • recover as debt from contractor (who 'pays')
24.3 • Employer to refund liquidated damages if architect fixes later completion date

CLAUSE 25: EXTENSION OF TIME
25.1 • Terms 'delay, notice and extension' include further instances
25.2 • Contractor to architect 'forthwith'
         • give notice to secure extension, when need 'apparent'
         • state causes of actual/anticipated delay
         • identify any relevant event
     • Contractor to architect at same time or 'as soon as possible'
         • set out effects
         • estimate delay and interrelation with other delays
     • Contractor to architect 'as necessary/as required'
         • further notices to keep up to date
         • material changes in effects and delay
     • Contractor to send copy to any nominated sub-contractor affected at each stage
25.3 • Architect to contractor
         • decide
             • there is relevant event
             • delay in completion likely
         • give extension on present data, stating
             • which relevant events covered
             • effect of any omission variations in reducing the extension

- this to be done
  - within 12 weeks of contractor's (original) notice, or
  - by completion date, if closer
  - subject to adequacy of particulars and estimates
- Architect to contractor may fix earlier completion date, provided
  - has already been extended
  - due to omission variations issued in meantime
- Architect to contractor within 12 weeks of practical completion finally to fix completion date which is
  - later date, by review of
    - relevant events, whether notified by contractor or not
    - previous decision or otherwise
  - earlier date, due to
    - omission variations issued since last extension
  - same date confirmed
- Provisos
  - contractor to
    - endeavour to prevent delay in progress and completion
    - proceed to architect's satisfaction
  - architect to send *every* nominated sub-contractor each amendment of completion date
  - no completion date fixed may be earlier than original completion date
- 25.4 • List of relevant events
  - *force majeure*
  - exceptional weather
  - clause 22 perils
  - industrial action etc.
  - some architect's instructions
  - late information from architect
  - nominated sub-contractors' and nominated suppliers' delay
  - work and materials by employer or others on his behalf
  - statutory action restricting labour, materials, fuel or energy
  - unforeseen shortages of labour or material
  - statutory work by local authority etc. or failure to perform
  - failure by employer to provide ingress or egress

COMMENTS ON CLAUSES 23–25

Normal progress and postponement

Clause 23 defines what is effectively a maximum contract period, although subject to extension of time under clauses 25 and 33. Within this period the details of how the contractor produces the works are left open. The requirement is that he shall 'regularly and diligently proceed' with the works. This does not exclude some variation in the pace of working, but guards against erratic and slow progress that would make completion even at any reasonable time after the completion date most unlikely. In these circumstances, the employer has the remedy of determination under clause 27.1.2.

The limited power of the architect to influence the speed or order of working has been noted under 'General considerations.' Specifically, he may only slow down work by postponement under this clause and the contractor cannot object to such an instruction or seek arbitration over it. He can however seek extension of time, payment for loss and expense or even determination against the employer (see Ch. 7).

Damages for non-completion

The architect's certificate is a condition precedent to the employer's right to damages under clause 24. It is a simple statement that the completion date has been reached with the works incomplete and it should follow hard on that date. No estimate of the likely date of actual completion is required. The completion date is the original date or that date as already amended under clause 25 and this applies until any later date is given under the procedure of that clause.

The general principles of liquidated damages are discussed in Chapter 1. This clause assumes that they have been calculated at a rate per period of time (which is usually per week) and allows for them to be secured from the contractor progressively if required but not in advance, either by deduction from certified amounts or other sums due or as a debt. If a retrospective extension of time gives a later completion date, so that the contractor has paid too much, the employer is to reimburse the contractor.

The contractor does not have to pay sums over automatically; he may wait until the employer acts. The employer in turn may wait until the final certificate under clause 30 and deduct or recover then, but not later. Often the sums will be deducted from the amounts of interim certificates. In the case of interim and final certificates, the architect and the quantity surveyor are involved in presenting the figures to the employer for payment, but they must *not* deduct sums for liquidated damages: it is only 'the employer (who) may deduct', as is discussed over all such amounts in 'Interim and final calculations' in Chapter 10. They should therefore advise the employer collaterally of his right to deduct any of the sums due.

The expression 'the whole or such part' of the damages takes account of the possibility of partial possession or sectional completion reducing the *rate* of damages due.

Contractor seeking extension of time

Clause 25 acts as a safeguard for both employer and contractor, by extending the completion date when particular causes of delay occur and by removing the threat of liquidated damages in those cases. How this may help each of the parties is discussed in Chapter 1. For an extension of time to be granted, there are two essential conditions: the right procedures must be followed under clauses 25.2 and 25.3 and the causal event must fall within the list in clause 25.4.

The contractor must act first under clause 25.2, or he will receive no extension. The architect is under no obligation to act or even to know that he might. There are two certain stages and a third possible stage in the contractor's action. In each case he must not act with promptitude, otherwise he may lose his right to an extension, as he may by waiting have denied the architect the possibility of taking action to avoid or mitigate the effects.

The first stage is that 'it becomes reasonably apparent' that a delay is actual or likely, when the contractor must explain the circumstances and cause and identify any 'Relevant Event'. Only events causing delay and included in the list in clause 25.4 qualify to secure an extension. It may be possible at the same time to take in *the second stage* of giving the effects and then estimating the delay; if not, this information must follow 'as soon as possible'. The first stage should not be held up until the second can be included: speed is of the essence. The second is often complicated, and so held up, by the need to take account of the various effects of other overlapping relevant events.

The third stage is to give any further information as a running review of a changing situation. This the contractor should do in his own interests, but the architect may ask for it to assist him in acting under clause 25.3, as he will be doing by this stage.

Architect granting extension of time

The architect's action is to respond to the contractor by granting an extension or, it may be inferred from the silence of the clause, by declining one. If he is satisfied in principle with the contractor's case in whole or part, he is to grant an initial extension within a time limit under clause 25.3.1 and to state his grounds, including the relevant events taken into account. The extension is effectively a minimum in that, when fixing the final completion date under clause 25.3.3 after completion has actually occurred, the architect can take the same or other relevant events into account only to fix a later date still. The architect may therefore wish to err on the conservative side in the initial extension granted, but must be careful as too low an extension could give rise to the contractor contending that he had been misled into some compression of his work. The only leeway that the architect has at the final stage is that he is reassessing at once *all* extensions granted and that if he decides to confirm the previous date he does not have to explain whether he has offset an increase against a decrease!

There is a further element in clauses 25.3.1 and 25.3.3, which also constitutes the whole of clause 25.3.2. This is the possibility of reducing an extension already granted or one currently being granted by taking account of any significant reduction in work content due to instructions omitting work. It is not possible for the architect to fix an earlier date on this basis before granting a first extension. This is in keeping with the stipulation in clause 25.3.6 that prevents a date ever being fixed that is earlier than the original date.

The two provisos in clause 25.3.4 are intended to avoid a delay becoming more extensive than it need be. Under the first, the contractor is to use his own initiative to minimise the effects, rather than passively sitting back while they build up. This is obviously in his own interests, since an extension of time is not necessarily accompanied by a loss and expense payment under clause 26 and the contractor will be out of pocket accordingly. He could also face an action from the employer for not proceeding diligently. Under the second proviso, the contractor is to respond to requests of the architect to keep the works moving. This is not a *carte blanche* to the architect to order extra overtime or massive reorganisation and indeed the clause gives him no power to instruct at all and gives the contractor no right to be paid anything extra. It envisages co-operation based on workmanlike activity and again on the balancing of financial interests by the contractor.

Nominated sub-contractors and extension of time

The special position of nominated sub-contractors in these conditions is highlighted by the requirement three times in clause 25.2 for the contractor to give copies of detail to any of them affected by a particular delay. The architect has to notify *all* nominated sub-contractors under clause 25.3.5 of extensions granted, but not give any supporting detail. This complements the position under clause 35.14.1 that the contractor cannot grant an extension to a nominated sub-contractor without the architect's consent and also the extension provisions, very similar in most respects to the present, in the sub-contract documents. These are referred to in both clauses 35.14.1 and 35.14.2 and require the architect to investigate any matter of extension for a nominated sub-contractor. While it is the contractor who fixes the extended date by notifying the sub-contractor, it is the architect who decides what it is to be. This is the case not only over the relevant events, but also for a delay to the sub-contractor caused by default of the contractor: the most significant additional element in the sub-contractor clause. Here the sub-contractor will receive an extension, but not the contractor. This draws the architect quite deeply into affairs that are far from design and largely within the contractor's own domain. It is also bound up with delay of nominated persons as one of the relevant events leading to an extension and discussed below. Domestic sub-contractors and even nominated suppliers do not share this special position and the architect has neither the opportunity nor duty to act.

The clause does not refer to the architect's 'fixing' of a date as certifying, so that the employer is not automatically notified. Since however an extension is modifying a major term of the contract, he should be.

Grounds for extension of time
The list of relevant events in clause 25.4 is the largest of three related lists in the conditions, the others being in clauses 26 and 28. Even so, it excludes other events by its very specificness. It falls fairly clearly into two categories of events:

(a) Those not due to either of the parties, but broadly to some outside agency's action or inaction. They do not lead to a loss and expense payment under clause 26 and only in a few cases, when severe, to determination under clause 28. This category is included primarily to protect the contractor against liability for damages.

(b) Those due to action or inaction of the employer or the architect. These may also lead to loss and expense payment and determination, although they are then more restricted in places, particularly over which architect's instructions qualify. This category is included primarily to protect the employer from facing the loss of a closely contained completion date. It is unfortunate that the architect has to act as judge and defendant over some of these issues, as happens in clause 26 also.

The various causes under the three clauses are grouped and

compared in Chapter 14, to bring out these distinctions. In no case is the contractor prima facie responsible for a relevant event, although there are some uncertain areas as noted under the individual events.

Force majeure. This makes the list 'open-ended', but only at the upper end of the scale by allowing for very severe happenings not specified.

Exceptional weather. Adverse weather, wet, dry, hot, cold or windy, is to be expected: it is the exceptional in intensity, extensiveness or timing that is allowable here.

Clause 22 perils. The further list in clause 1 of matters causing damage to the works needs little comment. It may be analysed into natural hazards, accidental effects of man's activities and less accidental effects. Sometimes the contractor may be in the chain of causation and the peril may even come about by the contractor's negligence, but there is no qualification here to avoid an extension, as there is to avoid a determination in clause 28.

Industrial action, etc. This brief title is not quite comprehensive. More importantly, the line extends right back through the production process to its source, giving a wide range of possible events.

Some architect's instructions. The clauses quoted refer to :

(*a*) The resolution of discrepancies or divergences, perhaps with additional work or with resultant waiting time.

(*b*) Variations and the expenditure of provisional sums, that is routine physical changes and developments.

(*c*) Postponement, not involving physical change.

(*d*) Action (and inaction) on the discovery of antiquities.

(*e*) Nominated sub-contractors and suppliers, particularly but not only over nomination, determination and renomination. Also there is:

(*f*) Opening up work, etc., where liability is apportioned as it is over the cost of making good in clause 8.3.

Late information from architect. The key point here is the time needed for the architect to prepare the information and then for the contractor to organise work or obtain supplies, so that the contractor must apply sufficiently ahead. But also he must not apply unreasonably early. This presumably is to prevent him contending that he needs information before he really does, to bolster up some form of claim. There is however a lot to said for the contractor asking for whatever he can as soon as he can, provided he schedules when 'due time' for receipt will be.

It may be that some of the information is due from a nominated sub-contractor or nominated supplier, but lateness in it reaching the contractor will still lead to an extension of time. In such a case, the use of the Employer/Sub-Contractor Agreement or the Warranty Agreement for a Nominated Supplier (see Ch. 5) enables the employer to claim against the person concerned, as the agreement includes liability for the design itself and its timing.

Nominated sub-contractors' and nominated suppliers' delay. This provision applies only to nominated persons, again as in a special position, and in this case it includes suppliers. As the contractor is responsible for delivering up the whole of the works on time, including those parts executed by nominated persons, and therefore for organising and progressing them, the wording is difficult. Firstly, it is likely from the view taken by the courts of 'delay on the part of' that this is to be limited to delay during performance by the person and not, for instance, to delay arising later due to defects and so 'caused by' the person. Secondly, if the nominated person can demonstrate that he delayed as stated and that the contractor pressed him, then not only is the contractor not liable to the employer, but the contractor cannot seek damages for delay from the nominated person, even though the separate question of loss and expense for disturbance may still arise. The employer in turn cannot act against the nominated person, as there is no direct contractual relationship. None of this gives the nominated person any great incentive not to fall behind.

The use of one of the agreements mentioned in discussing the previous relevant event overcomes this problem by giving the employer a direct route to secure redress from the nominated person, while keeping the contractor clear of liability. If one of these agreements is not used, the employer is at risk as he cannot recover. In any large or complex nomination, the architect should be sure that an agreement *is* used. The granting of an extension to a nominated sub-contractor under clause 35.14 certainly exonerates him from liability under the present heading, since such an extension can be granted only with the architect's consent. It will help the contractor as well if it is due to a relevant event but not, reasonably enough, if it is due to default by the contractor. The involvement of the architect in the granting of all extensions for nominated sub-contractors is therefore important to decide whether 'the Contractor has taken all practicable steps' to mitigate delay.

The whole arrangement here is somewhat circuitous. As indicated in Chapter 5 it is a concession to a person for being nominated, but also to the contractor for virtually having to accept the nomination, rather than make his own choice.

Work performed or materials provided by the employer or others on his behalf. If the employer unexpectedly introduces someone other than the contractor to perform extra work on the site, this may cause a delay to the contractor. A delay may also be caused if an expected person does not provide work and materials, so preventing the contractor from performing later work. Clause 29 permits the employer to bring on others by agreement, although it does not mention supply of materials which should be evident from fixing items in the contract bills.

Not only are there the cases of unexpected and deficient performance, but also there is the case of work that the contractor knows about and can allow for in the contract sum and in his programme and which is performed satisfactorily in manner and time. Such work is within the scope of clause 29 and strictly the present clause says too much by suggesting the possibility of an extension for such work.

Statutory action restricting labour, materials, fuels or energy. The action here can be very broad, but it must affect the contractor's own activities (which would include those of his sub-contractors) rather than suppliers, it must not have been taken before the date of tender (whenever its effects are felt) and it must be an act of central government and not of some other central body, even a national corporation.

Unforeseen shortages of labour and materials. Again the date of tender is the hinge point, in this case to determine whether the contractor knew then that the shortage was going to occur. If he could have known, he gets no extension. Here the test is 'inability for reasons beyond his control', which is more difficult to determine than direct statutory action. It must be quite a radical state of affairs and not just a case of having to go to an alternative and dearer or more troublesome source of supply. Fuels and energy are excluded in this case.

Statutory work by local authorities etc. or failure to perform. This provision does not cover work performed as a sub-contract, but work which the body has a statutory obligation to perform and which clause 6.3 excludes from being a sub-contract.

Failure by the employer to provide agreed ingress or egress through adjoining property. The property in question is not part of the site, which is given into the possession of the contractor. Here the contractor is granted only a right as set out in the contract documents to pass through at some 'due time', which may be for the whole contract period or quite brief. A special notice from the contractor may be a prerequisite to passage. The reference to 'ingress or egress as otherwise agreed' is difficult, as it suggests extension of time for a lapse in a post-contract agreement, which in turn suggests some adjustment of the contract terms.

SYNOPSIS OF CLAUSES 17, 18

CLAUSE 17: PRACTICAL COMPLETION AND DEFECTS LIABILITY

17.1 • Architect to certify practical completion, with deemed effects

17.2 • Architect to list defects etc. occurring in defects liability period
  • in schedule of defects
  • within 14 days of defects liability period ending
• Contractor to make good defects at own cost

17.3 • Architect may instruct defects etc. to be made good earlier
• Contractor to make good as before

17.4 • Architect to certify when defects made good

17.5 • Contractor liable for frost damage occurring *before* practical completion only

CLAUSE 18: PARTIAL POSSESSION BY EMPLOYER

18.1 • If employer takes early possession of any part with contractor's consent, several events follow
  • employer to certify estimate of approximate value of part
  • for several purposes practical completion of part occurs and defects liability period begins
  • separate certificate of making good defects to be issued
  • contractor to reduce insurance under clause 22A, if any
    • employer to assume risk
  • liquidated damages to be reduced proportionately

Note: the Sectional Completion Supplement, which is published separately from the contract conditions, produces a similar effect to clause 18 for *anticipated* early hand-over of part of the works. This is done by amendments to be read as incorporated into the conditions.

COMMENTS ON CLAUSES 17, 18

Practical completion and defects

There is no requirement for the contractor to apply for the practical completion certificate and practical completion is achieved under clause 17 when the architect is of the opinion that it occurs. This is when he considers the works to be complete in practical terms, although he has not checked in detail that everything is correct. The employer is then free to take possession and the architect has the defects liability period (usually inserted in the appendix as six months) in which to check the details while the building becomes operational.

The architect may no longer instruct the opening up or testing of work which does not appear defective, as he could during progress. He may deal simply with defects, etc. 'which shall appear', that is come to notice whether they were strictly visible before practical completion or not. What he has to do is to point out the defects, so that the contractor may decide how to put them right. As it was during progress, the method of producing the finished result specified is still up to the contractor. As he does the work without charge, it is important for this reason to leave the method to him. There is a rider about adjusting the contract sum if the architect instructs, but the circumstances in which this would happen are difficult to envisage.

Notification by the architect of defects is made in one of two ways, one being the formal schedule of defects under clause 17.2. Once this schedule is issued it ends the architect's power to bring the contractor back to make good defects, although the contractor remains liable for them in other ways for the period up to the final certificate under clause 30. The schedule therefore should not normally be issued until the end of the defects liability period and should include everything outstanding. If though there is any defect which it is required to have made good earlier (and the contractor has to act within a reasonable time), it is necessary for the architect to use the other approach of clause 17.3 and issue a separate instruction. What he must not do is to call this specifically a schedule of defects. The architect also has to make a distinction when listing defects between frost damage before and after completion: the idea is tidy enough, the verdict is the problem!

When the architect is satisfied that all defects are cleared, however notified to the contractor, he is to issue a single certificate of making good to tidy matters up.

The two certificates under this clause have various effects 'for all the purposes of this Contract' and these are as follows:

(1) CERTIFICATE OF PRACTICAL COMPLETION

(a) Beginning of the defects liability period under clause 17.2.
(b) Liability for frost damage under clauses 17.2, 17.3 and 17.5.
(c) End of insurance of the works by the contractor under clause 22A, if applicable.
(d) End of liability for liquidated damages under clause 24.2.1.
(e) End of regular interim certificates under clause 30.1.3.
(f) Halving of the retention under clause 30.4.1.3.
(g) Beginning of the period of final measurement under clause 30.6.1.2.
(h) Opening of arbitration on most matters under article 5.

(2) CERTIFICATE OF MAKING GOOD DEFECTS

(a) Release of the second half of the retention under clause 30.4.1.3.
(b) One element leading to the final certificate under clause 30.8.

Partial early possession
The comments here may be taken as also applying in principle and where suitable to the Sectional Completion Supplement (see Ch. 2), which can be used as an additional part of the original contract, the main difference being in whether a progressive hand-over was included at the contract stage or not.

Clause 18 is only valid when the employer takes possession 'with the consent of the Contractor'. To enter otherwise is a breach of clause 23. It is practicable for both physical and legal reasons to exercise partial possession only in respect of a distinct entity within the contract, such as a whole building or at least a whole wing. This is particularly true over liability for damage occurring before practical completion of the whole works.

The architect is to certify 'the total value of the relevant part' based on an approximate estimate (see Ch. 15), which should be as close as is reasonable in the circumstances in view of the three uses to which it is put:

(a) to lead to a reduction in retention under clause 30.4.1.2,
(b) to reduce the value of the works insured by the contractor, if under clause 22A, but he must assess the sum here,
(c) to reduce the rate of liquidated damages applicable to work not yet complete.

Of these three uses, the first two are effected by a direct reduction. The third is to be by calculating a ratio and applying this to the rate of liquidated damages. The ratio is that of the contract sum reduced by the estimate of value as the one part, to the contract sum as the other part. Provided that the final account for the works (without the inclusion of fluctuations) comes out close to the contract sum, this gives a balanced result. If elements like variations and adjustment of prime cost sums produce a substantial swing either way, the effect on the portion of damages remaining may be significant.

The other consequence of partial possession under the clause is to introduce an early defects liability period and making good of defects for the part concerned, by activating parts of clause 17. This is based on a 'deemed' practical completion only for these purposes and for the first reduction of retention, and not a 'full'practical completion leading to all the other consequences listed under clause 17. At the appropriate interval there is to follow a certificate of making good defects, when the further reduction of retention occurs for the part of the work.

Partial possession may take place more than once in the course of the contract, as the opening words of the clause recognise, and the various events of this clause will run as series, overlapping as may be necessary and perhaps also with sectional completion.

CHAPTER 7

DISTURBANCE OF PROGRESS OF THE WORKS

GENERAL CONSIDERATIONS

The clauses considered in this chapter touch on four ways in which the progress of the works may be disturbed, rather than simply delayed:

(*a*) Loss and expense to the contractor may be caused by matters which disturb progress and which are in essence the responsibility of the employer or architect. This issue is the subject of clause 26 and may flow from some of the same events as lead to extra time under clause 25, although an inevitable joint invoking of the clauses every time must not be assumed. The causal matters in clause 26 are all contained in clause 25, but there are less of them in view of their more limited scope (see comparison table in Ch. 14). The clause is providing a remedy for acts and omissions, most of which are breaches of contract, but it does not preclude the contractor from using the other remedies available. The clause assumes that, whatever the extent of disturbance, somehow the works will reach completion.

(*b*) Either party may be so affected by one of a number of matters as to act against the other to bring work under the contract to a premature end and to recoup his loss. The term used in both clause 27 (where the employer acts) and clause 28 (where the contractor acts) is 'determine the employment of the contractor', so that in either case it is the activity of the contractor that ends. The *contract* is not determined, as this would end all recourse to its provisions (including those in clauses 27 and 28!) to help wind matters up. Instead it is only the *employment* of the contractor that is ended, leaving the contract otherwise in being to be wound up on the basis given, although again this does not remove from the party invoking the clause concerned the right to other remedies. The reasons given in the clauses for acting are quite drastic and therefore few: there are several matters each constituting a breach by the other party, there is the insolvency of the other party and there are several major external influences affecting the contractor by causing severe delay. When the contractor determines due to such delay, the reasons again include a small selection of the events listed in clause 25, but not identical with those in clause 26 (again see comparison table in Ch. 14). The details of the clauses assume that the contractor does not return to complete work, although there is a passing reference in the former of the clauses to the possibility of a reinstatement.

(c) Hostilities and war damage may affect the parties adversely. This may be on account of the physical or financial difficulties of carrying on the contract, of the undesirability or illegality of completing during wartime, or of war damage occurring. Clauses 32 and 33 provide several routes in these circumstances, although how far they will be followed in practice may be wondered. They both envisage the possibility of completion or of earlier determination at the option of either party.

(d) Interesting or valuable objects, new or old, may be discovered and they may warrant holding up the works while they are investigated in position, since moving them may reduce their special status. Clause 34 gives a wide power to the architect in these circumstances, with a reimbursement provision for the contractor. Extension of time is covered in clause 25.

Clauses 26, 27 and 28 all embody the reservation that they are 'without prejudice to any other rights and remedies' which the aggrieved party may possess. They are intended to provide a formula for settlement and usually will suffice, but the parties may still resort to arbitration or the courts. This may be instead of using the relevant clause, especially if some other issue is involved, such as a point of law. But it may also be after trying the clause and finding it wholly or partly wanting or after plainly failing to reach an agreement. It may be conceded that clauses 32 and 33 are quite likely to be insufficient in the circumstances they envisage, and perhaps irrelevant as well.

SYNOPSIS OF CLAUSES 26–28, 32–34

CLAUSE 26: LOSS AND EXPENSE ETC.

26.1 • Contractor may apply to architect
  • stating
    • direct loss and expense occurred/likely to occur.
    • which 'matter(s)' causing
  • when
    • regular progress materially affected
    • no other contract reimbursement covers it
  • If architect forms opinion that progress affected, to
    • ascertain amount of loss and expense, or
    • instruct quantity surveyor to do so

- Provisos, contractor to
    - apply as soon as possible
    - furnish information as requested to establish architect's opinion
    - furnish details of loss and expense to permit ascertainment
26.2 • List of 'matters'
    - late information from architect
    - opening up or testing, when work in order
    - discrepancies or divergences
    - work and materials by employer or others on his behalf
    - postponement of work
    - failure by employer to provide ingress or egress
    - variations and provisional sum expenditure
26.3 • Architect to state any extension of time granted for particular relevant events
26.4 • Contractor to pass on any similar application by nominated sub-contractor
    - Architect to deal with it similarly to one by contractor
    - Architect to state any extension of time likewise
26.5 • Any amount ascertained to be added to contract sum
26.6 • This clause without prejudice to other rights and remedies

CLAUSE 27: DETERMINATION BY EMPLOYER

27.1 • This clause without prejudice to other rights and remedies
    - Architect may give contractor notice of any of these defaults
        - total suspension of works
        - irregular with works
        - deliberate non-removal of defective work or materials
        - unapproved sub-letting
    - Employer may determine contractor's employment within 10 days, either
        - if contractor continues default for 14 days after architect's notice, or
        - if contractor later repeats same default for any length of time
27.2 • If contractor becomes insolvent etc.
    - employment of contractor automatically determines
    - but may be reinstated by agreement
27.3 • (Not used in private edition): relates to 'Corruption' in local authorities edition
27.4 • When employment of contractor determined, rights and liabilities of parties
    - employer may engage others to complete works with him

- they may
  - use contractor's temporary items on site
  - use contractor's materials on site
  - purchase further materials necessary
- except on contractor's insolvency
  - contractor to assign agreements with suppliers and sub-contractors to employer
    - subject to their reasonable objection
  - employer may pay suppliers and sub-contractors for materials and work
    - before/after determination
    - if not paid by contractor
    - this being additional to provisions regarding nominated sub-contractors
- Contractor to remove all his temporary items from site
  - when architect requires, but not before
  - otherwise employer may sell them in reasonable time
    - holding net proceeds for contractor
    - without responsibility for loss or damage
- Contractor to pay/allow employer direct loss and damage due to determination
- Settlement between parties to be net difference
  - by employer
    - what would otherwise have been paid without determination
  - by contractor
    - what paid to him before determination
    - what paid by employer after determination
    - loss and damage incurred by employer (for which contractor is declared liable)
  - until completion and settlement of accounts, employer not bound to pay contractor anything on account

CLAUSE 28: DETERMINATION BY CONTRACTOR

28.1
- This clause without prejudice to other rights and remedies
- Contractor may forthwith determine his own employment by notice to employer or architect, if
  - employer defaults on honouring certificate and continues default after due notice
  - employer affects due issue of certificate
  - suspension of whole/most of works occurs for named period due to
    - *force majeure*
    - clause 22 perils, unless contractor etc. negligent

- civil commotion
- some architect's instructions
- late information from architect
- work and materials by employer or others on his behalf
  - opening up or testing, when work in order
- employer becomes insolvent etc.

28.2 • Without prejudice to various rights and remedies, already accrued or arising by injury during removal
- contractor to remove temporary items and materials from site
  - unless paid for by employer
- employer to pay contractor, so far as not already paid, for
  - work completed before determination
  - work commenced before determination
  - loss and expense incurred before determination
  - materials ordered or for which contractor must pay
  - cost of his removal
  - loss and expense due to determination, including that of nominated sub-contractors
- employer to notify contractor and nominated sub-contractors of apportionment of amounts between them

CLAUSE 32: OUTBREAK OF HOSTILITIES

32.1 • Either party may determine employment of contractor forthwith
- if
  - outbreak of hostilities occurs, and
  - general mobilisation occurs
- provided
  - 28 days have elapsed
  - not after practical completion, subject to war damage

32.2 • Architect may within 14 days of determination instruct contractor to perform
- protective work
- work up to points of stoppage
- provided contractor able to complete within 3 months
  - otherwise he may abandon work

32.3 • When contractor finally stops work
- clause 28.2 to apply for settlement
  - except for loss and expense due to determination
- protective etc. work to be valued as variation

90 PART 2 — CONTRACT CLAUSES

CLAUSE 33: WAR DAMAGE
33.1 ● If war damage occurs
    ● contractor to be paid for works themselves, as though it had not occurred
    ● architect may instruct
        ● removal of damaged work
        ● execution of protective work
    ● contractor to comply and complete works
        ● subject to extension of time
    ● extra work to be valued as variation
33.2 ● If war damage occurs and followed by notice of determination under clause 32
    ● protective work already instructed to rank as instruction after the notice
33.3 ● Employer to receive any compensation payable
33.4 ● 'War damage' defined

CLAUSE 34: ANTIQUITIES
34.1 ● All such objects found during progress to be property of employer
    ● Contractor to
        ● cease work to extent necessary
        ● preserve object in original position and condition
        ● inform architect or clerk of works
34.2 ● Architect to instruct contractor on actions
    ● Contractor to permit third party to examine, remove etc.
        ● such party to be employer's responsibility
34.3 ● Architect to decide whether loss and expense
    ● Architect/quantity surveyor to ascertain amount
    ● Architect to state to contractor any related extension of time
    ● Any amount to be added to contract sum

COMMENTS ON CLAUSES 26–28, 32–34

Loss and expense of the contractor
The purpose of this clause is to reimburse the contractor when he would not be 'under any other provision in this Contract', so that it covers costs not allowable under such arrangements as those over variations in clause 13. It thus deals with what are quite often known as 'claims'. It is not however an open cheque to cover all eventualities and some are the contractor's liabilities, such as the cost of adverse weather, and some must be dealt with by court

action, such as failure to give possession. It certainly does not allow the contract sum to be set aside and 'costs' to be substituted. These points are made clear by two considerations relating to clauses 26.1 and 26.2. One is that 'the regular progress' is 'materially affected' by one or more of the restricted list of matters given. These matters are a reduced set of those in clause 25 and need no further comment, beyond noting that the responsibility for them lies with either employer or architect and that this is the reason for paying for their consequences (see comparison table in Ch. 14). These restricted matters must lead to the restricted result of significantly affecting progress. They do not result in works which look physically different after completion, and they are not relevant for this clause if they solely result in other expense, such as buying in a dearer market or losing some discount. There must be disturbance of progress. This means either breaks in progress or changes in order of working, in any case of 'material' extent. The establishment of a right to an extension of time does not necessarily mean that there is a right to extra payment here (although it will usually help), and the reverse argument does not follow inevitably either.

The other consideration is that what the architect or the quantity surveyor has to do is to 'ascertain the amount of such loss and/or expense', that is the extra cost of disturbance irrespective of the price level of the works proper contained in the contract sum. To calculate the amount as the difference between the contract sum and the actual cost of the works to the contractor could be unfair to either party, as this approach involves reassessing everything by substituting a prime cost basis. On the other hand, some recent legal decisions have allowed a profit margin (or even interest) on the amount, which used not to be permissible.

The procedure for the contractor to be reimbursed is similar to that for him to receive an extension of time. He has to initiate matters by stating the fact of disturbance, present or pending, and the causal matter but not necessarily giving an amount initially. It is for the architect to form an opinion on the justification of the contractor's statement in principle, which is often making him both judge and defendant again, as with clause 25. He should base this on any available evidence; the conditions provide for nothing specific, except possibly the contractor's master programme in clause 5, which need not be presented or revised so as to be suitable. Once he has formed his opinion, either he or the quantity surveyor is to settle the amount. Of the three provisos, the most important is for the contractor to give early warning, as it is often difficult to weigh up the effects unless they can be observed when they occur. Failure on his part here will tell against uncritical acceptance later of any of his figures for which evidence is lacking and so may lead to a lower settlement. It also prevents the architect taking any avoiding action, by way of instructions to reduce the extent of loss and expense.

Clause 26.3 requires the architect to give any information about extension of time that is relevant here. This would take any aggregate extension and divide it into the parts attributable to relevant events which did and did not also rank as 'matters' under this clause. It does therefore appear to forge some inferential direct, if unexplained, link between extension and loss and expense.

Clause 26.4 effectively applies all the foregoing to nominated sub-contractors, whose sub-contracts contain similar clauses and require the architect or the quantity surveyor to ascertain the amounts. These sub-contracts also contain provisions about claims between the contractor and the sub-contractor, and relating to default by one of them. Here the architect and the quantity surveyor are not required to intervene, which stands in distinction from the parallel sub-contract situation over extension of time where the architect *must* give his consent.

The whole clause is rounded off with an authority to adjust the contract sum, and so also pay amounts on account, and with the provision of the 'without prejudice' statement discussed earlier in this chapter.

Determination of the contractor's employment

Clauses 27 and 28 have important similarities in structure and differences in operation. Both proceed through causes, determination, subsequent actions and settlement of liabilities and both have the 'without prejudice' reservation just mentioned as occurring in clause 26. Major differences are:

(*a*) The employer has to give notice prior to determination except when the contractor is insolvent, while the contractor has to do so in one instance only.

(*b*) Determination on the insolvency of the contractor is given as automatic, although this may not be legally valid, but with an option of reinstatement if this turns out to be workable. If the employer becomes insolvent the contractor must act to secure a determination, but it is then final.

(*c*) When the employer determines, there are provisions about completing the works since these effect final settlement between the parties. This question is irrelevant in the other case.

(*d*) Terms of settlement are more favourable in tone when the contractor determines.

Under clause 27 the matters of default by the contractor are all contraventions of the conditions. The first two are against clause 23.1 and are represented by a withdrawal of men and by a dilatory approach, so that the completion date or anything reasonably near it is clearly unobtainable. The third offends clause 8.3 and applies to a major cause where it is physically impracticable to bring in others under clause 4.1.2 to remove the defective work or materials while the contractor is in possession. The last is self-explanatory.

Under clause 28 the employer may be at risk in two ways relating to certificates, the first being the one case in the clause when he receives warning. In the case of non-payment the reference is to 'amounts properly due', that is amounts calculated in accordance with the conditions by the architect or the quantity surveyor and shown in the architect's certificates. The term might or might not be held by the courts to allow for those deductions which the employer is permitted to make under various clauses from the certified 'amounts properly due'. If it were not (and the point cannot be pursued here), then strictly the employer risks a determination if he deducts his entitlements. The deductions in question are summarised in Chapter 15. The second instance is that in which the employer tries to influence the architect over a certificate, which need not be one for payment alone.

Then there are a number of causes of suspension leading to a possible determination. The length of suspension is to be inserted in the appendix and is usually put as one month for most causes, but three months for clause 22 perils. The material points in the causes are discussed under clause 25 (see also comparison table in Ch. 14). The significant difference in two cases here is the exclusion of the cause if it is itself due to negligence of the contractor. This could have been done in the other clause, but presumably is here because of the more drastic consequences of determination.

Completion after the employer determines
Clause 27.4 allows for the employer having the outstanding works performed by others, or even by his own direct labour. No particular method is given and he may do whatever is in his interest in the circumstances to balance money and time, so long as he exercises reasonable commercial prudence. To facilitate this, those carrying out work may use the contractor's temporary buildings, plant etc. without charge to them or to the employer. These items are to be released for the contractor to remove when the architect so authorises, which may be progressively as they become superfluous. They may become a liability if not removed upon request and so can be sold if needs be, although the

employer is not responsible for loss, any more than he is for fair wear and tear. The contractor is entitled to receive the net proceeds, which therefore are *not* put into the final accounting, as would be more beneficial to the employer if the contractor is insolvent and cannot pay his ultimate indebtedness in full (see financial example in Ch. 14). Hired plant etc. does not come into these arrangements at all and hire firms may remove such items after determination, unless the employer or his new contractor enters into further independent agreements.

Materials on site are available for incorporation into the works without charge and so help to reduce the likely indebtedness of the contractor. This is intended to be so whether the contractor has paid for them or not, but several legal decisions indicate that this is a difficult area relating to the adequacy of the title which the contractor has acquired. Further materials may be purchased as needed.

To help secure continuity, the contractor must be prepared under clause 27.4.2 to assign his supply and sub-contract agreements to the *employer*, if these are likely to be required. This is a holding operation until any new contractor is appointed, when an assignment to him in turn may occur. The persons whose agreements are being assigned are obliged to accept the first step blindly and so the right to reasonable objection to the second is included here. Further, the employer has the option but not the duty, to pay such persons sums not paid by the contractor. This applies whether or not there is an assignment and whether or not the contractor was due to have paid at determination; in fact it extends to materials delivered after determination, in the confused period that often ensues. Neither the right to accept an assignment nor that to make payment exists, however, when there is insolvency of the contractor. If the employer tries to act here he is likely to run into trouble with the liquidator or the like and perhaps end up paying out twice. Even without this he is not obliged to make payments in most cases, and it may be a question of goodwill or inducement to maintain continuity if he does.

Settlement under clause 27.4.4 is a question of ascertaining the difference between all the amounts that the employer has paid or suffered as losses and what he would have paid had the determination not occurred. Most of the amounts are straightforward. There are the net payments actually made under interim certificates, while the general retention is retained by the employer to offset other amounts. Nominated sub-contractors' retention is not available to the employer and must be paid out to the persons concerned when it becomes due. There are all the completion payments, including new contracts, materials and so forth paid for and extra fees produced by the extra activities of consultants. But there is also loss and damage, which increases the effect of delay, assessed on its own merits and not by directly applying the rate for liquidated damages, as clause 24 has lapsed with the determination. To arrive at what would have been paid it is necessary to prepare a hypothetical final account for the contract, which involves translation of instructions and so forth (especially over defective work, etc.), recalculation of amounts and quite a bit of care in reconstructing some events.

In the end the difference becomes payable usually, but not always, from contractor to employer. If the contractor is insolvent (and this may have happened *after* determination) the employer receives whatever proportion is available, so underlining the care to be exercised in making extraneous payments at determination. It may be observed that a precise account for the value of work and materials at determination is not needed in these calculations at any stage, although one may sometimes be useful for collateral purposes.

Lastly, the clause provides that the employer does not have to make any payment to the contractor between determination and settlement, if anything is due. He should not even honour any interim certificate in his hands on the day of determination. But equally the employer also will not receive anything during the same period and this will add to his expense and to his problems.

Arrangements after the contractor determines

Under clause 28.2, arrangements are limited to the departure of the contractor and his payment. The contractor is under an obligation to remove all that is his from the site as soon as is reasonable. A strict reading of the clause may well allow him to remove even materials which the employer is to become liable to purchase, but has not yet purchased, under clause 28.2.2.4. As he evacuates, he is to take such precautions as necessary to prevent injury etc. to persons and property. This takes the place of his clause 20 indemnities, now lapsed, and gives the employer a right of action but more limited protection. There is no obligation to perform any work to prevent deterioration of the works, or even to leave the works in such a condition as not to be a source of injury. The employer, liquidator or the like must act quickly here.

Settlement consists of paying the contractor for what he has done and lost. In this case a precise account of work complete and incomplete at determination *is* needed, and this is to include materials. These are those materials on site or ordered, such that the contractor is bound to pay for them, but would not include any excess of materials as these would not be 'properly ordered'.

The other activity of the contractor is the cost of removal, allowing this either as actual cost or as a proportion of any identifiable prices in the contract bills.

The contractor's loss is given as two elements. Normal 'direct loss and/or expense' is that occurring entirely before determination,' even if ascertained afterwards, and due to the usual causes. Special 'direct loss and/or damage' is that occurring entirely at or after determination and includes loss of anticipated profit on work not carried out by the contractor.

Nominated sub-contractors are specifically mentioned here; their amounts occur within various parts of the accounts and the duty falls on the employer under clause 28.2.3 to give the separation between them and the contractor. Nominated suppliers, domestic sub-contractors and others also come into the reckoning for at least some of the elements of settlement, but here the contractor is to sort out the amounts with them himself.

Hostilities and war damage

Clauses 32 and 33 warrant only outline comment, both because of the uncommonness of their use and the likely inadequacy of their · provisions. During hostilities the parties may simply proceed to completion, but if either chooses to determine, events and liabilities under clause 32 follow the same pattern.

This pattern is similar to that of clause 28, when the contractor determines against the employer, but it is softened for the employer in three ways. Under clause 32.1, there are the two provisos limiting when determination can be notified, although it still occurs 'forthwith' when it is notified. Under clause 32.2, the contractor may be required to perform limited work to ensure that the works have reached reasonable points and are protected against the ravages of time while incomplete. He is protected by a time limit on such activities, although he need not abandon work then. Lastly under clause 32.3, while clause 28.2 is introduced as the direct formula for settlement, with the addition of protective and other work after determination, it is tempered by the exclusion of loss and damage due to the determination. Thus the contractor is paid for all that he does, including removal from site, but any loss due to the onset of hostilities remains with the party incurring it.

War damage may accompany determination due to hostilities, and either may precede the other, although only determination after damage is mentioned in clause 33. The procedures given suit either order, however. Clause 33.1 is worded as though no determination has occurred and its provisions follow the pattern in clause 22B: removal of work affected, protective work, reinstatement and payment for this extra work. A simple fixing of a later completion date is required, without any notice or other procedures and without any review. This is the only extension of time provision outside clause 25.

The events of clause 33.1 may be interrupted by determination and clause 33.2 allows any suitable requirements under clause 33.1 to be considered as under clause 32.1, so that matters can be brought to a tidy stage on cessation of the work. Clauses 33.3 and 33.4 need no comment.

Antiquities, etc.

Objects unexpectedly discovered on site may be intrinsically valuable, interesting by virtue of their position or possibly both. Clause 34 provides for them to be the employer's property, subject to any question outside the contract of treasure trove, and requires the contractor automatically to take the three steps of care, preservation and notification. Involved in these steps is the obligation to stop work if this is necessary to prevent disturbance.

The architect has to act after these emergency steps by giving instructions and no limit is set on their nature. They may therefore include the contractor allowing a third party on site to investigate and perhaps remove the objects, and also performing extra work which would be valued as a variation. This work might extend to co-operation with the third party, but would not bring the contractor into any responsibility for him, as is specifically stated. Beyond the direct cost of work specially performed, there may be loss and expense. Here the clause follows clause 26, but without elaboration of detail. The contractor does not have to give notice that loss and expense is likely and the matter lies directly with the architect. There is no limiting criterion of disturbance of regular progress, although this is the most likely cause in the circumstances. Also the requirement for the contractor to provide details in support of amounts is not given, although this is bound to happen. The statement about extension of time is however parallel to that in clause 26, as is the provision for adding the amount to the contract sum and so to interim payments.

CHAPTER 8

INJURY TO PERSONS AND PROPERTY

GENERAL CONSIDERATIONS

This chapter is limited by the term 'injury during progress', as are the three clauses considered, but the term may be taken to embrace a number of issues:

(a) Injury is to persons and property.

(b) In the case of persons, death is taken in as well.

(c) In the case of property, the works themselves are included.

(d) The effects of injury are covered, and they may include consequential further injury (possibly after practical completion) and consequential direct loss.

(e) The prevention of injury, its mitigation and restoration so far as possible are included.

(f) The resulting liabilities of the parties and of others come into the reckoning.

These threads may usefully be followed through the clauses as minima. The clauses have a closely related progression, based on their underlying philosophies:

(a) The contractor is to indemnify the employer against the consequences of events brought on by the carrying out of the works and causing injury. Indemnity is the protection which one party to an agreement gives the other against a particular loss or against the claims of a third party. It might appear that if, say, the contractor injures a person passing the site that he alone will be liable. But in particular circumstances such a person may be able to bring an action against either or both parties to an agreement, if he is injured by virtue of its performance. The direct acts of the one have been induced by the other. Clause 20 requires the contractor to indemnify the employer very widely in scope and without limits to the liability that may come about. It does not require the employer to indemnify the contractor, although it does limit the contractor's indemnity in some cases.

(b) The weakness of the contractor's indemnity may be that he does not have the resources to meet his liabilities. Clause 21 therefore requires him to maintain particular categories and levels of insurance to meet claims accordingly. The insurance is his first port of call in a claim but, if it turns out to be too narrow in scope or inadequate in amount, the contractor remains liable to the employer under the indemnity for the balance. The presence of insurance does not release the contractor from his basic position of indemnity.

(c) There are also particular injuries to other property, usually buildings near the works, which may be a risk because of the intrinsic nature of the works, even if the contractor proceeds in accordance with the contract and without negligence. Clause 21 also deals with these cases by requiring a special insurance in joint names to protect both employer and contractor against claims arising, but only when the contract bills specifically call for it.

(d) There are some hazards which are removed from both indemnity and insurance by clause 21. These are matters where no insurance is obtainable, although nuclear risks are the responsibility under statute for compensation purposes of those perpetrating them.

(e) The contractor is liable to deliver up the works complete under the contract and for all costs of achieving this, including reinstatement after damage, since the contract is 'entire' (see Ch. 1). His indemnity given under clause 20 includes the works so far as they are damaged by reason of carrying them out. There are however other perils that may damage them and clause 22 provides for insurance against such damage to back up the contractor's capacity to meet his liability. This is done by using three alternative versions, clauses 22A, 22B and 22C, to provide for these options:

(i) New works, with the risk and insurance carried by the contractor.
(ii) New works, with the risk and insurance carried by the employer.
(iii) Works of alterations or extension to existing structures with the risk and insurance of new and existing structures and contents of the latter carried by the employer.

It is particularly significant that the risk passes to the employer in cases (ii) and (iii), so that if the insurance fails the employer will bear the cost of reinstatement.

(f) In works of alteration or extension, there may be damage to both new and existing premises. If so, the contractor is required to reinstate only the works, it being possible that the damage to the existing may be so great or affect work of such a character, that it would be beyond the range of the contractor or would change the scope of work beyond what the contract envisages. But it is also possible that the works cannot be reinstated unless the existing is reinstated first, because the one is contained or supported by the other. Even more fundamentally, faced with substantially destroyed premises, the employer may wish to complete the destruction and have something different built. For these and other conceivable reasons, or so it may be conjectured, the conditions allow either party to seek to determine the contractor's employment, subject to a right to arbitration by the other. What happens to the insurance settlement then falls out of the present picture. There is also the possibility of damage to the existing structures, while the works are untouched. This is not mentioned, as the contractor does not have to reinstate. The employer might want to determine in such a case and he would have to settle as best he might.

(g) Nothing is said about loss or damage suffered by the employer, other than over fees. Almost certainly there will be an extension of time if there is a major incident affecting the works, so that he will suffer a delay loss unless he insures specially.

This outline does indicate a logical progression, but it also suggests the possibility that one piece of injury or one cause may overlap with another. To reduce the problems that may result it is as well for as much insurance as possible to be placed with the same insurer, preferably on the contractor's running all-risks policy.

The passing of *risk* to the employer under clauses 22B and 22C is a serious matter and these clauses should be used sparingly. Clause 22B can be recommended only when the employer is himself an insurer or can obtain unusually favourable terms. Clause 22C is inevitable for the type of work that it covers. It is possible in a contract covering both new work and alterations or extensions to use clauses 22A and 22C for the respective parts, provided that they are physically distinct entities, to avoid doubt about which insurance is in question if there is damage.

SYNOPSIS OF CLAUSES 20–22

CLAUSE 20: INJURY TO PERSONS AND PROPERTY AND EMPLOYER'S INDEMNITY
- Contractor liable and indemnifies employer
  - against liability, loss etc.
    - due to carrying out works
20.1 - regarding personal injury or death
  - unless due to employer's etc. negligence etc.
20.2 - regarding injury to property

- provided due to contractor's or sub-contractor's negligence etc.
- except when covered by clauses 22B or 22C

CLAUSE 21: INSURANCE AGAINST INJURY TO PERSONS AND PROPERTY

21.1
- Contractor and sub-contractors to insure
  - against clause 20 liabilities
  - without prejudice to indemnity under clause 20
- Level of insurance to be
  - statutory, where a contract of service
  - for sums in appendix, otherwise
- Contractor and sub-contractors to satisfy architect that insurance in force
  - usually by documentary evidence
  - specially by policies and receipts
- Employer may insure to extent of any default
  - and deduct from money due to contractor
  - or recover as debt

21.2
- Contractor to insure in joint names of employer and contractor
  - when provisional sum in contract bills
  - for amount there stated
  - *re* damage to property other than works
  - against risks of collapse etc caused by works
  - when employer may be liable
  - but excluding
    - negligence of contractor or sub-contractors
    - and other matters listed
- Architect to
  - approve insurers
  - keep policies and receipts
- Amount expended to be added to contract sum
- Employer may insure to extent of any default, as before

21.3
- Excluded from the contractor's indemnity and insurance regarding property
  - radioactive and nuclear matters
  - aerial pressure waves

CLAUSE 22: INSURANCE OF THE WORKS AGAINST CLAUSE 22 PERILS

22A.1
- Contractor to insure in joint names of employer and contractor
  - for reinstatement value, and any fees stated
  - regarding damage to works and materials on site
    - but not to temporary buildings, plant etc.
  - against clause 22 perils

- footnote: so far as possible
- until practical completion

22A.2
- Architect to
  - approve insurers
  - keep policies and receipts
- Employer may insure to extent of default, as before

22A.3
- Alternatively to 22A.1, contractor may
  - utilise running policy to provide cover
  - provided employer's interest endorsed on policy
- Contractor to satisfy architect that this insurance in force
  - usually by documentary evidence
  - specially by policies and receipts
- In default, clause 22A.2 to apply

22A.4
- Contractor to
  - restore work and remove debris
    - upon acceptance of insurance claim
  - and proceed to completion
- Contractor to
  - receive all insurance money, except fees
    - through architect's certificates at time of interim certificates
  - but no other money

22B.1
- Employer to carry risk
  - regarding damage to works and materials on site
    - but not to temporary buildings, plant etc.
  - by clause 22 perils
- Employer to insure against risk
  - footnote: so far as possible
  - producing policy and receipt to contractor on request
- Contractor may insure to extent of any default
  - and have amount added to contract sum

22B.2
- Contractor to give notice to architect and employer
  - of loss or damage
  - giving extent etc.
- Contractor to be paid for works themselves, as though damage not occurred
- Contractor to
  - restore work and remove debris
  - be paid for extra work as variation

22C.1
- Employer to carry risk
  - regarding damage to
    - existing structures and contents
    - works and materials on site
  - but not to temporary buildings, plant etc.
  - by clause 22 perils

- Employer to insure against risk
  - footnote: so far as possible
  - producing policy and receipt to contractor on request
- Contractor may insure to extent of any default
  - being allowed to enter existing structures for survey
  - and have amount added to contract sum

22C.2
- Contractor to give notice, restore and be paid as clause 22B.2
- Subject to option that
  - either party may determine employment of contractor
    - within 28 days of loss or damage
  - either party may request arbitration
    - within 7 days of determination notice
    - as to justice of determination
- If arbitration upheld
  - clause 28.2 to apply
  - except loss and damage due to determination

COMMENTS ON CLAUSES 20–22

Injury to persons and property in general

Clauses 20 and 21.1 are closely linked, the former giving the contractor's liability of indemnifying the employer and the latter the insurance requirements to back this up but, as explained, not to take its place. Both parts of clause 20 are similarly structured and very wide-ranging, but with limits that may be noted:

(a) The indemnity is one way, from contractor to employer only.

(b) Injury etc. arises only from carrying out the works and not from defects in what is produced.

(c) For injury to persons, the act or neglect of the employer, etc. is excluded.

(d) For injury to property, the neglect, omission or default of the contractor must be involved.

(e) For injury to property, the works themselves are excluded when the employer specifically carries the risks named under the other clauses, but no further.

The results of defects and other bad performances by the contractor under (b) may form the subject of action for breach, if they occur completely distinctly, but the position is not simple. The difference between injury to persons and property means that the burden of proof shifts: in (c) the contractor must prove the employer's liability so as to be relieved himself, while in (d) the employer must prove that of the contractor. As there are various intervening areas of liability where neither party has been negligent and so forth, it may not be enough for a party simply to demonstrate his own lack of negligence. Someone has to take the liability when the works are quite deliberately being produced.

The insurance of clause 21.1 is 'without prejudice' to the indemnity. It extends to similar insurance by all sub-contractors against whom the contractor or his insurers would have recourse if once a claim against the contractor justified it. The standard obligatory forms of nominated sub-contract and the standard optional form of domestic sub-contract each contain clauses to suit. Over employees etc. the clause simply reminds the contractor of his statutory obligations, while in the case of other personal claims and those over property the minimum amounts of cover are prescribed and are to be those included in the appendix. Both parties need to view these amounts carefully and the contractor may well carry a higher level in his running cover anyway.

Clauses 21.1.2 and 21.1.3 are repeated in clause 21.2 and in the options of clause 22 with some variation on the theme. In each case the employer is given safeguards against a failure of the contractor to insure and given the right himself to insure and cover a complete or partial gap. To detect any lapse, the architect needs a right to check up and he is given this, with safeguards for the contractor against officiousness. The employer may deduct the expense of insurance from payments he makes to the contractor or otherwise act to recover it. The measure is what he has paid and not what the contractor would have paid or did in fact include in the contract bills.

Special injury to property
Clause 21.2 stands aside from the clauses so far commented upon, by dealing with a situation in which the contractor carries out the works quite properly, in that he performs them as contract, and yet the very performance results in damage to other property. The damage is given by the clause quite specifically as collapse and several other contingencies having a structural effect. If the contractor uses a particular working method by way of, say, piling, de-watering or sequence of demolition that has been specifically required of him by the contract documents, then he is not liable if he is not negligent and damage still occurs. On the other hand the employer is, because he has commissioned the works. This is a very special insurance to cover very serious risks and a very expensive one, so that it is dealt with differently from all the other insurances in these clauses.

The approach is to include a provisional sum in the contract bills, as the contractor cannot price in advance for this insurance. Without this provisional sum the insurance does not arise at all, although it could be introduced by agreement of the parties if the sum were accidentally omitted. The architect is to approve the insurers in this instance as well as, by implication, the policy and is to retain the policy and the receipts. As the precise risks may not be established until the contract is placed, this pattern allows the architect close involvement in the negotiations and allows the contractor to be reimbursed for the actual amounts he pays. To guard against an aggrieved person or even the insurer proceeding against the person who is not insured, the insurance is to be in joint names.

The list of excluded causes of damage has little contractual significance: it will be rehearsed in the policy and it does not put any liability on the contractor by being given in the clause. Negligence of the contractor has been mentioned and the other causes are clear. In the case of faulty design, the employer should proceed against the architect. The difficulty may be in distinguishing in practice between faulty design and faulty execution.

If under clause 21.2 the contractor fails in insuring, the employer still insures, but here just does not pay the contractor. No deduction is needed.

Clause 21.3 brings in the uninsurable exceptions mentioned at the beginning of the chapter and applies them for clauses 20 and 21. The definition of the clause 22 perils deals with them for all parts of clause 22.

Injury to the works
Several elements of clauses 22A.1 and 22A.2 (taken together), 22B.1 and 22C.1 are similar:

(a) The value to be insured in each case is that of reinstatement, and so is to be taken at current costs and not at contract bill prices, which would be dated and also inadequate for clearance and possibly piecemeal work. Only in the case of clause 22A.1 when the contractor insures, are professional fees included. In the other cases the employer should cover them anyway.

(b) Cover is limited to the works and materials on site, and the contractor's temporary items are explicitly excluded. So implicitly are materials off-site; when any of these have been paid for the contractor is made responsible for insurance under clause 16.2. The cover is for 'all work . . . and materials' and so must include that of sub-contractors, nominated and domestic. The various standard sub-contracts state that this is so and that sub-contractors need not insure.

(c) The contractor's liability to insure ceases at practical completion under clause 22A.1. No limit is given under the alternatives, where insurance must run just as long to satisfy the contract, but sensibly will continue beyond to protect the employer. Equally he will insure from completion onwards when clause 22A.1 is used.

(d) The clause 22 perils, defined fully in clause 1, apply in each case. The list gives the major accidental and natural hazards in normal insurance terminology and makes the same standard exclusion as clause 21.3. In some cases, an accidental hazard may arise out of the performance of the works or even because of negligence of the contractor, but the insurance still covers this. The contractor also receives any consequent extension of time under clause 25 in this case, whereas clause 28 excludes a peril from the causes of determination if the contractor is negligent. The list also includes the deliberate acts of riot and civil commotion, but it excludes other acts in this category such as theft and vandalism, which the contractor should cover. The possibility of not always being able to obtain insurance against all of the perils is recognised by the footnotes and the parties should take appropriate action.

(e) If the responsible party fails to insure, the other may do so and recoup his expense. The employer has the stronger incentive to make up the contractor's deficiency since, if there is serious delay due to damage, there can be a determination under clause 28. Here the contractor is paid in full for leaving, while the employer receives only the insurer's money with which to carry on, if he so wishes. If a failure to insure by either party might lead to insolvency, this is however a strong incentive for the other to insure to be certain of payment.

There are several differences between these clauses:

(a) Only when the contractor insures is the insurance to be in joint names. This has the advantages already discussed, in particular that of avoiding the insurer proceeding against the non-insured party on the basis of negligence. It would be very helpful to the contractor under the two alternative clauses, if it were required there also.

(b) The risk passes with the insurance to the employer in the latter two alternatives, this has been commented upon earlier in the chapter.

(c) Approval of the insurers and depositing of the policy and receipts is required only in the first alternative, when the contractor insures. Otherwise the policy is to be 'proper' or 'adequate'. In the last alternative, the contractor has a right to survey if he needs to insure on the employer's default; this could be an onerous task to undertake and no reimbursement is provided.

(*d*) When the contractor insures, there is the option of using the contractor's all-risks policy to meet the obligation, by endorsing the employer's interest for the limited purpose of the contract. The policy becomes in joint names to that extent and may be so endorsed concurrently for a whole range of employers on various contracts. There is no power to approve the insurer and only a limited power to inspect the policy and receipts, but still a power to insure if the contractor defaults. This option is the one most frequently used, because of its convenience.

Clauses 22A.4, 22B.2 and 22C.2 deal with events if loss or damage occurs, and have several similarities:

(*a*) Each requires the contractor to restore the works, remove debris as he goes and then proceed to completion. Under clause 22A.4 restoration is to commence as soon as the insurance claim has been accepted, while in the other two cases not even this usually brief pause is indicated. The method of restoration is not mentioned: it is at the contractor's discretion, so long as he still produces the finished works as specified and to that extent under the architect's surveillance. There is likely to be an extension of time granted.

(*b*) The contractor is entitled to extra payment for the extra work and delay costs. In the case of clause 22A.4, the amount is that of the insurance settlement, apart from the fees element that goes to the employer, and the contractor receives neither more nor less. In the other two cases, the contractor is paid as though the work is a variation instructed by the architect, so that payment for any direct loss and expense follows accordingly. Only under clause 22C.3 are actual instructions needed, these being for removal of debris which may include that from the damaged existing structures. The insured party should therefore ensure that the settlement is adequate as a lump sum, or otherwise that it progressively matches the actual costs incurred.

(*c*) Payments to the contractor are made progressively. When the employer has insured and because they are then variation amounts, they simply go through the interim certificates and will be subject to retention. Under clause 22A.4 they are made under separate certificates of the architect at the same time as the interim certificates, because they are made from a joint holding account that receives the insurer's payments. As such they should not carry retention. There is no proper argument for it in the other cases, as the retention has already been held on the work when first carried out, but variations attract retention.

There are two differences under these settlement clauses:

Only when the employer insures does the contractor have to give notice of loss or damage, since he will himself claim when he insures. However, the major difference is the option for either party to determine the employment of the contractor under clause 22C.2, following the timetable given. (Determination in other circumstances is considered in Ch. 7.) The grounds for this are 'if it is just and equitable', a pretty open statement which leaves little guidance for the arbitrator to whom one party may request the other to go. There need not be any arbitration of course, if the parties agree to the determination in the first place. Presumably any arbitrator is to weigh considerations such as those outlined in the opening part of the chapter. The question of undue delay as a ground for determination is covered by the main determination provisions in clause 28. In view of this ground, the arbitrator must act fairly quickly as a delay in his award does not suspend the main right of determination.

If there is a determination the contractor is to remove and be paid in accordance with clause 28, that is as though he had determined, but without allowance for loss and damage due to the determination itself.

CHAPTER 9

VARIATIONS AND FLUCTUATIONS

GENERAL CONSIDERATIONS

That the contract sum may be adjusted only when the conditions permit it has been explained in Chapter 3, in dealing with clause 14.2. The various authorisations throughout the conditions for adjusting the contract sum are listed in Chapter 15, and it may be noted that in principle they can be put into three groups:

(a) Those reflecting a change in the works forming the subject of the contract, either in their physical nature or in the required manner of performing them.

(b) Those recompensing the contractor for some expense caused (usually) by the employer or the architect, but without any change in the works, although some disturbance may be provoked.

(c) Those taking account of market and other costs of inputs affecting the cost to the contractor, again without any change in the works.

These groups do not include value added tax, which is dealt with under the supplementary agreement and not as adjusting the contract sum.

This chapter deals with the first and last of the groups by taking clause 13 on variations and provisional sums and clauses 37–40 on fluctuations. The other instances are dealt with in the relevant chapters, although some reference to the question of loss and expense is needed here also for completeness. It is convenient to take clause 13 alone in detail and then to take the other clauses together and in less detail in this introductory guide. Any further points that might have been given here are given under the respective comments, since they are quite distinct and relate fairly closely to the contents of the clauses.

All adjustments are drawn together in a final account in preparation for the final certificate. Both of these documents are considered in the next chapter.

SYNOPSIS OF CLAUSE 13

CLAUSE 13: VARIATIONS AND PROVISIONAL SUMS
13.1 • Variation has two sides to meaning
   • both change what in contract bills
   • first changes what on contract drawings also
   • First, change in physical works
      • addition or omission of work
      • alteration of materials
      • removal of work or materials properly on site
   • Second, change in working restrictions
      • access to and use of site
      • working space, hours and order
   • It excludes substitution of nominated work for work measured and priced by contractor in contract bills
13.2 • Architect may instruct variations
   • Architect may sanction variations introduced by contractor
   • Variations required by architect do not vitiate contract
13.3 • Architect to instruct about expending provisional sums
   • in contract bills
   • in sub-contracts
13.4 • Variations and expending provisional sums to be valued by quantity surveyor
   • in accordance with clause 13.5 for contractor
   • in accordance with nominated sub-contract for nominated sub-contractors
   • unless otherwise agreed by employer and contractor
   • If prime cost sum arises from provisional sum and contractor's tender accepted
      • rules therein apply instead
13.5 • When possible valuation to be by measurement
   • using contract bill prices for
      • similar character and similar conditions
      • non-significant change in quantity
   • using derived prices for
      • dissimilar conditions
      • significant change in quantity
   • using fair prices for
      • dissimilar work
   • Omissions to be valued at contract bill prices
   • In any valuation
      • measurement to follow principles of contract bills
      • percentage and lump adjustments to be allowed
      • preliminaries (if appropriate) to be allowed
   • When measurement inappropriate

- value by daywork
  - prime cost as defined
  - percentage additions as contract bills
  - similarly for specialist trades
  - vouchers for labour, plant and materials verified weekly
- If conditions of unvaried work affected by a variation
  - work to be treated as if varied, and
  - revalued as variation
- Fair valuation to be made if
  - variation is not of work, added or omitted, or
  - liabilities associated with variation require it
- No loss and expense allowance to be made here
  - if covered elsewhere

13.6
- Quantity surveyor to allow contractor to be present at measurement to take notes
- Effect to be given by adjusting contract sum

COMMENTS ON CLAUSE 13

The scope of this clause is given by its title and the definition of 'Variation' in clause 13.1. It relates only to variation of firm quantities, although incidental provisional quantities in firm bills can be dealt with by regarding them as broadly equivalent to provisional sums. The first side of the definition of variation relates to changes in the works as included in the contract. These may be changes in arrangement, quantity or specification instructed before work is performed, but may also be changes after work is performed and so leading to demolition and other removal. In all cases they change the work physically and no particular limit is put on what may be changed, since in each of the cases given the word 'any' occurs.

The second side of the definition relates to changes which do not affect the finished works, but rather the means of achieving them, and here quite definite limits are imposed on what may be changed. These are delineated by the four matters of access, space, hours and order as given. While each of these relates to some aspect of organising the works, none of them is in itself a directly time-related matter, although a change here may result in the fixing of an amended contract date. Not only is there a limited list of matters, but also the authority given by the clause is to change only what is imposed in the contract bills. If therefore there is, for instance, no limitation on working hours in the bills the architect is not empowered to instruct one. As the four matters permit of some overlapping in practice, the insertion of one in the bills may lead to a resultant necessary adjustment of another on the contractor's part and so come within the variation adjustment. The word 'addition' must be taken as 'addition to' obligations and restrictions already imposed to yield a consistent meaning here.

The term 'Variation' is to 'exclude' a particular case of nomination: this is to act as a prohibition on what the architect may do. If there is work measured in the contract bills as contractor's work, this may not be removed from the contractor and given to a nominated sub-contractor without any change in its character. This is quite distinct from omitting such work and substituting different work which is that of a nominated sub-contractor. This is inevitable in the ebb and flow of variations and is not usually something done solely for commercial or quality control reasons. Even here, a substantial shift in emphasis may entitle the contractor to a revaluation under later provisions of this clause.

A variation may be introduced by an architect's instruction under clause 13.2 or by him sanctioning what the contractor has already done. The contractor has no authority under the conditions to vary anything (emergency work under clause 6.1 is perhaps the nearest approach) and, if he attempts to do so, the architect may instruct him to remove work under clause 8.4. However, this retrospective action of the architect can be useful to mop up items that often crop up somehow, perhaps by a clerk of work's 'direction' that has been obeyed. The other way that a variation may come about is by one of the 'as if it were' provisions in the conditions, under which something is deemed to be a variation without the need for an instruction. One occurs later in this clause and they are all listed in Chapter 13, along with some other matters that lead in effect to a variation.

No variation is to vitiate the contract. This time-honoured negative provision adds little to what is expressed before positively. It remains true though that a mass of individual variations can wreck the intention of a contract quite effectively. If this happens, it is necessary to use generously the terms of this clause about similar conditions and changing the conditions of other work in order to achieve a sensible valuation. To the extent that regular progress has been disturbed, but not otherwise, clause 26 may also come into play.

There is however the distinction between 'variations within a contract' and 'variation of a contract' mentioned in Chapter 1 to consider. The former is what this clause envisages, that is relatively incidental changes that still leave the works the same in character and scale. If it were proposed to change the works from, say, a block of flats to a factory, this would constitute variation of the contract. So too would increasing from one block of flats to two. In each case there is a fundamental change in the subject-matter and the contractor is not obliged to accept this, whether he is capable of the work or not. A variation of the contract by proposing to reduce from two blocks of flats to one is different in that the employer must always have the right to have work left out. Here the contractor might be entitled to rescind the contract and sue accordingly, unless adequately revised terms were agreed.

Provisional sums are simply sums already included in the contract with some definition of their purpose, so that there is an allowance for expenditure still to be decided. The architect has a duty under clause 13.3, rather than an option as with variations, to instruct on expending them. In this instance some or all of the work may legitimately turn into nominated work and this is allowed for in clause 35.1 where nomination is defined. When the instructions are once issued, the rules for valuation of variations and provisional sum expenditure are the same.

The authority for valuation is in clause 13.4, and its main thrust is for the quantity surveyor to value in accordance with the rules, either in clause 13.5 or in nominated sub-contracts. Work put out to a domestic sub-contractor is valued still as the contractor's work for this purpose, so that any difference in terms is entirely between contractor and sub-contractor. There are two exceptions to the main rules. The employer and the contractor may agree to some other basis, which they may do as the parties to the contract even without it being said. This stipulation is most likely to be used if there is some self-contained additional item, such as a large joinery fitting or a car park, for which the employer seeks a special quotation from the contractor before deciding to authorise it via the architect. The other exception is that of nominated work arising out of a provisional sum, for which the contractor's tender is accepted. This may contain other rules and these are to be followed. Such a tender can also come about in relation to a prime cost sum without any provisional sum under clause 35.2, which introduces similar arrangements.

The rules of clause 13.5 are set out in an order of priority for use. Clauses 13.5.1–13.5.3 covered measured valuation. In the case of additions, bill prices, pro rata prices and star prices (as they are usually called) are to be resorted to in turn by observing the criteria of character, conditions and quantity as given. Some prudence is needed here to offset one small distinction against another and so avoid endless adjustments. The term 'fair rates and prices' suggests a level of pricing equivalent to that in the contract bills and inclusive of a reasonable profit margin, even if the original pricing was net of profit. In the case of omissions the bill prices are used. In both cases, the measurement principles are to be as used for the contract bills. Any percentage or lump adjustments included in the contract bills, such as for insurances and errors, must be applied in the valuation, whereas adjustment to preliminary items may or may not be needed, depending upon the scale and nature of variations etc.

Direct measured valuation may not be adequate for several reasons. While it is almost always possible to measure work, it is not always possible to price it. For this situation, clause 13.5.4 allows for daywork, which is priced at rates current when it is performed under the definitions given. Clause 13.5.5 reintroduces measured valuation in a roundabout way. The direct valuation of additions or omissions may be quite adequate, but related unvaried work may also be affected by changed conditions. Thus it may become or cease to be possible to use the same scaffolding for work of several trades, or work may become more or less piecemeal or accessible. The clause therefore allows such work to be revalued as though it has itself been varied, without the need for a further instruction. It may also be necessary to use this provision to revalue unvaried work if the 'significant change in quantity' provision comes into play under clause 13.5.1, so that the same rate applies to both varied and unvaried work.

Lastly and negatively, direct measured valuation is unsuitable by definition for elements of cost that are quite unmeasurable. Clause 13.5.6 defines these negatively. Positively its provisions would apply to such cases as variations in obligations and restrictions under clause 13.1.2 where the effect is spread quite widely across operations, or to special administration or supervision associated with an otherwise measurable variation. No rules are given and a fair valuation is to be made, that is inclusive of a normal profit margin.

The proviso at the end of clause 13.5 excludes any loss or expense allowance from the application of this clause. It is to be allowed, if appropriate, under clause 26. This means that pricing here is to done as though there is no disturbance effect, although allowance may be made for work performed out of sequence, for example, so that there is small-scale working but with adequate warning. This may be a rather academic distinction and in practice the whole calculation can be done in one. The authority for the elements of calculation lying in different clauses is the key point here.

Two procedural points are given in clauses 13.6 and 13.7. The contractor is entitled to be present (presumably on site) to take notes of measurements, something of an understatement of the reality. Pricing points do not necessitate this. Then there is the regular authority to adjust the contract sum to allow for variations made.

SYNOPSIS OF CLAUSES 37–40

CLAUSE 37: CHOICE OF FLUCTUATION PROVISIONS
37.1 • Appendix to indicate which of the next three clauses applies
37.2 • If no entry made, clause 38 applies

CLAUSE 38: CONTRIBUTION, LEVY AND TAX FLUCTUATIONS
This clause is not given in detail, as it is completely contained within the fuller clause 39 following.

CLAUSE 39: LABOUR AND MATERIALS COST AND TAX FLUCTUATIONS
39.1 • Basis of contract sum and adjustment regarding wages etc.
   • prices in contract bills (including some insurances)
      • based on wages etc. for
         • workpeople on site
         • contractor's own workpeople not on site
      • in accordance with
         • rules etc. promulgated at date of tender
         • bonus schemes defined
         • holidays agreements promulgated at date of tender
      • and upon contributions etc. based on foregoing
   • if any increase or decrease
      • promulgated after date of tender
      • net amount added or deducted
   • for non-workpeople on site
      • proportionate amounts to be paid or allowed
      • at craftsman's rate
   • prices in contract bills based on
      • transport charges listed in contract bills
      • fares in accordance with rules etc. promulgated at date of tender
   • if any increase or decrease after date of tender
      • in transport charges
      • in rules or fares
      • net amount added or deducted
39.2 • Basis of contract sum and adjustment regarding contributions etc.
   • prices in contract bills based on
      • tender types and tender rates
         • all by statute
         • at date of tender
      • refunds of these
   • if any increase or decrease after date of tender

- net amount added or deducted
- for non-workpeople on site
  - proportionate amounts to be paid or allowed
  - at craftsman's rates
- contracted-out employment to count as equivalent to foregoing

39.3 - Basis of contract sum and adjustment regarding materials, electricity and fuels
  - prices in contract bills based on
    - market prices in 'basic prices' list
    - current at date of tender
    - fuels only if allowed by contract bills
  - if any increase or decrease after date of tender
    - net amount added or deducted
  - 'market prices' include duty or tax

39.4 - In domestic sub-contracts similar terms to clause 39 to be incorporated
  - Net amounts of adjustments then added or deducted as before

39.5 - Procedures and stipulations
  - contractor to give notice
    - of any event leading to an increase or decrease
    - within reasonable time, as condition precedent to payment
  - quantity surveyor and contractor may agree any net amount finally
  - amounts may be added to or deducted from
    - contract sum
    - determination amounts
  - contractor to provide
    - evidence and computations as required
    - certificate regarding domestic sub-contractors' evidence
  - no change in amount of profit to result from adjustments
  - no addition or deduction to be made
    - in interim amount or final certificate
      - for event occurring after completion date
    - provided
      - clause 25 applies unamended
      - architect has dealt with all fixings of completion dates

39.6 - Clauses 39.1–39.4 not to apply to
  - daywork
  - nominated sub-contractors and nominated suppliers

- work by contractor against prime cost sum
- changes in VAT

39.7 • Definitions
- date of tender
- materials and goods
- workpeople
- wage-fixing body

39.8 • Percentage stated in appendix to be added to
- amounts paid or allowed by contractor
- except for domestic sub-contract amounts

CLAUSE 40: USE OF PRICE ADJUSTMENT FORMULAE

40.1 • Contract sum to be adjusted in accordance with
- provisions of clause 40 itself
- formula rules
- Definitions in the formula rules apply here
- Adjustments to be made in all certificates for payment
- Correction to be made in next certificate

40.2 • Interim valuations to be made for each interim certificate

40.3 • Articles manufactured outside the United Kingdom to be dealt with by
- list of market prices attached to contract bills
- net addition to or deduction from these prices

40.4 • Nominated sub-contracts to be adjusted in accordance with their terms and formulae
- Domestic sub-contracts to have suitable provisions incorporated

40.5 • Quantity surveyor and contractor may change methods for calculating amounts, provided
- expected amount same or approximately same
- does not affect amounts for sub-contractors

40.6 • If monthly bulletins delayed
- fair basis of adjustment to be used
- If monthly bulletins recommence
- adjustments under these to be substituted for temporary
- During delay methods to be used to facilitate these adjustments

40.7 • If contract not complete by completion date
- index numbers when should have been complete to be used thereafter
- provided
- clause 25 applies unamended
- architect has dealt with all fixings of completion dates

40.8 • List of deemed amendments to formula rules

COMMENTS ON CLAUSES 37–40

Principles of the clauses

Clause 37 signals the selection of one clause from the alternatives that follow. If the appendix is not completed, the fail-safe provision selects clause 38. It is not the intention of the contract that no fluctuations shall apply, although it would be possible to delete all the clauses concerned, including clause 37 itself. The scope and method of the substantive clauses may be outlined to establish their uses.

Clause 38 allows for adjustments to be made to the contract sum to cover fluctuations in the costs incurred by the contractor in respect of outgoings (and occasionally refunds) originally introduced and then changed during the contract by some government action. These are referred to as forms of 'contribution, levy and tax'. It is because these are quite outside the operation of ordinary market forces and essentially unpredictable by the contractor, that clause 37 provides for clause 38 to operate as a minimum requirement.

The elements to which the clause applies fluctuations are labour, materials and goods, electricity and fuels, but only so far as the cost of these is affected by a change of tax etc., and in some cases only so far as they have been listed in the contract documents as admissible. No other causes of changed costs such as wage rates and transport operation are admissible, subject to the comment about consequential effects made under the clause itself. The method of calculating fluctuations, as distinct from the rules and what is allowable, is not set out in the clause but it is necessary to take man-hours, quantities of materials and other directly ascertained inputs to the works and calculate fluctuations on the basis of these amounts. The method therefore is based on the prime cost incurred by the contractor, so that the precise amounts of fluctuations are dependent on the working method of the contractor (whether, say, he substitutes plant for labour) and his efficiency in keeping his prime costs down, or otherwise. As such, it contrasts with the method in clause 40. It is the stated intention of the clause not to change the amount of the contractor's profit, a point discussed later.

Clause 39 includes all the government-related elements of clause 38 and embodies the same method of calculation. Its terms of reference however are given as 'labour and materials cost and tax fluctuations' so that it covers many more costs, but still includes electricity and fuels, not mentioned in the title. These are the market costs of the various inputs such as wage rates and the prices of materials, with again a list in the contract documents covering scope and in some cases the price levels on which the contract sum is based. The method of calculating fluctuations here is, like that of clause 38, by direct reference to the contractor's costs. As these are more extensively defined, the level of reimbursement is even more dependent on the contractor's relative efficiency.

Clause 40 proceeds on a quite different basis from the others. It is related to a separately published set of formula rules which define the technicalities of the system and which are incorporated into the contract by the reference made. These divide building work into a large number of categories, for each of which monthly bulletins published nationally give an index number representing the relative current average cost of that category of work based on actual tenders submitted. The contract sum is held to be based on the level of index numbers at the date of tender and fluctuations are calculated as the difference between these numbers and those applying at the time of the interim certificate in which work is first included, subject to some provisos. To operate on this basis, it is necessary for the contract bills to be analysed so as to break down into parcels of work corresponding to the formula categories. As the index numbers reflect the commercial situation each month, fluctuation adjustments can be viewed as taking account of all the elements covered by clauses 38 and 39 and all other inputs as well. But further they also reflect the degree of keenness of tendering at particular periods other than that of the contract tender and include the relevant profit margin. They therefore include a margin of profit as the other fluctuations professedly do not. Because they *are* related to index numbers calculated on statistical data, the fluctuations are not affected by any inefficiency of the contractor, an advantage, and indeed may misrepresent his efficiency, a disadvantage, both for the employer. They are a cruder approach in some ways for both parties, but save work on balance in their calculations. It is not appropriate in the present work to consider the details of the method further, as these pass out of contract into procedures.

From these outlines it may be seen that clause 38 is intended for relatively steady, or at least predictable market situations, and so for what are often termed 'limited fluctuations'. The other two clauses give what are then termed 'full fluctuations'. It has been indicated that it is possible, although contrary to intent, to have no fluctuations. This may be suitable for small projects of short duration under steady conditions. A middle approach would be to use clause 38 for, say, labour and clause 39 for the other elements or vice versa, in particular economic conditions. Clause 40 cannot be used in any way whatever with the others, nor does it permit any tampering with its mechanism.

As clause 38 is contained entirely within clause 39, as indicated in the Synopsis, it is easier to deal with the latter first.

Full fluctuations based on costs

Clauses 39.1 and 39.2 for labour and related expenditure and clause 39.3 for materials etc. each have a basic structure indicated by their identical opening sentences, that is a definition of the basis of prices leading to the contract sum and of the events that lead to a fluctuations adjustment. Within this structure there are also some side issues.

The key principle governing labour fluctuations in clause 39.1 is that the deemed basis and the adjustments are related in most cases to the provisions of the nationally recognised working rules and similar codes and the decisions over levels of emoluments under them. If a rule is itself changed this may change what the contractor pays, while a change in a wage or other rate established within the framework of the unaltered rules will have a similar effect. Either of these qualifies as causing a fluctuation. The clause gives three types of direct payments by the contractor: wages etc. bonuses and holidays schemes. Bonuses are mentioned separately, because the contractor is not obliged to pay them. Not only is there adjustment for these, but also for two other indirect types of payment which vary with them: employer's and third party insurances and contributions, levies and taxes payable as an employer. These indirect payments are related to the direct payments mostly on a percentage basis, so that an increase in direct payments consequentially increases what is payable for the others, even though the rate of insurance, tax etc. remains unchanged.

A subsidiary principle in clauses 39.1.1 and 39.1.2 is the distinction between 'promulgated at the Date of Tender' used there and 'current at the Date of Tender' (or similar) used elsewhere. The effect of the term 'promulgated' is that the contractor must allow in the contract sum for the effect upwards or downwards of a rule etc. properly made or changed at the date of tender, even if its financial effect is not to occur until later. He therefore only has an adjustment made for any later change.

A further subsidiary principle is the limitation as to which persons count for labour fluctuations. The primary group is 'workpeople', defined in clause 39.7.3 by reference to their wages being fixed by a wage-fixing body. Workpeople count if they are on site or not on site, the qualifications 'engaged' and 'directly employed' attached to these two varieties being uncertain in intent, since workpeople of domestic sub-contractors are covered by virtue of clause 39.4. For persons on site only who are not workpeople, some allowance is made by clauses 39.1.3 and 39.1.4, by stipulating craftsman's rate whatever the actual wage or salary may be and requiring at least two full days in a week to qualify. The last parts of clause 39.1 (clauses 39.1.5 and 39.1.6) take the fresh topic of transport and fares. The latter are dealt with by reference to rules and promulgation again. The former are covered by requiring a list of 'basic transport charges' to be given by the contractor. These charges are by inference in the class of being current at the date of tender, as they must be increased or decreased after that date to qualify.

Clause 39.2 deals with statutory impositions and refunds, which are defined comprehensively by clause 39.2.6 and 39.2.8, although clause 39.2.2 excludes training board levies. Clause 39.2.1 recognises a 'tender type' as the payment in principle and a 'tender rate' as the level at which it is set, both being as at the date of tender. The abolition of a type, the creation of a new one, or a change in rate all qualify under clause 39.2.2 as fluctuations. Clauses 39.2.4 and 39.2.5 deal with refunds in the same way. In between, clause 39.2.3 brings in allowance for non-workpeople in a similar way to that in clauses 39.1.3 and 39.1.4 for wages etc. Clause 39.2.7 brings in workpeople proper who are in contracted-out pension schemes that do not fall within the compass of a wage-fixing body and that otherwise would not qualify for fluctuations purposes.

Clause 39.3 deals with materials, etc. by means of a list of 'basic prices' on the same principles as the list of transport under clause 39.1. These prices are to be the market prices at the date of tender, so that a fluctuation in market price evidenced by invoice can be allowed fairly. There are a number of complications over materials prices in particular, as these can vary between suppliers so that careful definition is needed in the original list to avoid confusion over adjustments. The clause defines 'market price' as inclusive of duty or tax, so that the statutory element may be allowed as inclusive of a change at any stage of the production process. This is as well since only one price usually occurs on an invoice. The scope of items allowable under this clause is dependent on the length of the basic list and a balance needs to be struck to permit reasonable adjustment and to avoid undue work in making it. Fuels in particular may only be included when the contract bills say so, which really means when the tender bills say so or the contractor requests their inclusion at the contract stage.

The clauses so far considered apply for the contractor's own work, directly executed. If a domestic sub-contractor is employed, the contractor is required by clause 39.4 to incorporate similar clauses in the sub-contract. The use of Sub-Contract DOM/1 facilitates this. Only if this is done may the contractor be allowed fluctuations under this contract and, equally, be due to pass them on to the sub-contractor. Obviously the sub-contractor will press for the appropriate terms in the usual circumstance of fluctuations resulting in a net increase.

The rest of clause 39 moves on to matters other than the basis for calculating fluctuations. Clauses 39.5.1 and 39.5.2 require the contractor to give prompt notice of an event leading to a potential fluctuation. This may permit the architect in some cases to introduce a variation or other instruction that will reduce the impact of the fluctuation. For this reason such notice is made a 'condition precedent' to the contractor receiving an increase, but not to allowing a decrease! Under clause 39.5.3 the quantity surveyor and the contractor may arrive at figures which are binding on *both* parties, so that arbitration is precluded, and which figures are at their discretion as to the method of calculation.

Several accounting matters follow. Clause 39.5.4 gives the usual authority to adjust the contract sum and also the amount when the contractor determines his own employment. If the employer determines this authority is not needed, although a similar notional amount will have to be allowed. Clause 39.5.5 requires the contractor to produce 'evidence and computations' in support of fluctuations amounts. These will mainly be wage sheets, invoices and the like, but they are to be supplemented by certificates relating to non-workpeople.

Clause 39.5.6 makes the statement about the contractor's profit not being altered by fluctuations adjustments, reinforcing all the preceding references to 'the net amount of . . . increase or decrease'. Clause 39.8 however provides for a percentage addition to the various amounts 'paid or allowed', without any indication of the reason. It does mean that a suitable percentage or percentages will make up in a crude way for fluctuations in elements of cost not covered otherwise, such as the extra cost of non-workpeople above craftsman's rate, plant and overheads. As this *is* a crude approach it may be conjectured that it is sometimes a vehicle for a concealed profit margin!

Clauses 39.5.7 and 39.5.8 legislate for fluctuations adjustments, whether increase or decrease, to be frozen in part if work continues past the completion date. The extent of freezing is that no adjustment is to be made for an *event* which occurs after the completion date and which would otherwise lead to an adjustment. Adjustments due to previous events may however continue to grow. This freezing is subject to clause 25 being fully in force and the architect playing his part in fixing completion dates.

There remains several clarifications and definitions in clauses 39.6 and 39.7, most of which need no comment beyond any reference already made. Daywork is excluded from fluctuations adjustments because it is priced under clause 13.5 at rates current when it is performed. The date of tender is defined as ten days ahead of the date for receipt, so that the contractor when preparing his tender does not have to make adjustments to allow for changes in cost right up to the last minute. This does mean that tenders may not include some major increase 'promulgated' in the ten-day period, which should be borne in mind when tenders are assessed.

Limited fluctuations based on costs
The smaller scope of clause 38 has been delineated under clause 37 and few comments are needed. While no fluctuation in amount of tax etc. is allowable simply as a consequence of a fluctuation in wages etc., if the *rate* of tax fluctuates then the fluctuation is calculated in relation to the changed value of wages. Because clause 38.1.8 is shorter than 39.2.7, a fluctuation in pension contributions is restricted there to the lower 'deemed' state level.

For materials, etc. the principle of what is allowable is clear. It may be difficult to work out in practice, as invoices usually do not show the breakdown between various causes of fluctuations, especially those early in the chain of production.

Full fluctuations based on formula
This clause is considerably shorter than its alternatives, as the underlying definitions and procedures are in the formula rules and the direct calculations are limited to taking work at contract prices and using the index numbers. It does not even begin 'the Contract Sum shall be deemed' as this information is in the rules, as is the definition of the date of tender as ten days before the date of receipt, the same time as in the other fluctuations clauses. The timing of this date may affect which is the base month for the contract in a close case. At the other end of the process, the authority to adjust the contract sum is not given here, although it does appear in clause 30.6 about the final account.

It is however stated in clause 40.1.3 that adjustment is to be 'effected in all certificates for payment', which covers interim certificates and the final certificate. To enable this to work it is necessary for clause 40.2 to make interim valuations mandatory before each interim certificate. These valuations are to contain the amounts of work in each category and the adjustments due to changes in the index numbers and they are to be calculated at the appropriate time in the monthly period to ensure that work relates to the correct bulletin. In the case of a few days' shift of date and a large shift in an index number, incorrect application could be quite significant in its effect.

Even when the timetable is applied strictly, there may be inaccuracies in the actual calculations. Clause 40.1.4 allows 'correction of amounts' under formula rule 5 in the next certificate. These corrections are of arithmetical errors and of mistakes in allocations to work categories and in using index numbers. This last also covers the substitution of firm index numbers for the provisional ones that an earlier bulletin may have contained. Any correction of a quantity of work from one valuation to another is however expressly excluded. If therefore a quantity is low for instance, it will attract the relevant index numbers; next month any additional quantity will be included with the quantity omitted before, but the *whole* of this quantity will be taken in relation to the new index number. Greater accuracy than is normally needed for interim purposes alone is called for here, as the figures are final. Interim certificates run regularly until the one immediately after practical completion: any quantities thrown up during the period following are to be dealt with by an 'averaging' method under the rules, so spreading the effect back through the contract period.

Clauses 40.1 and 40.2 contain all the main provisions, when read with the formula rules. The rest of clause 40 deals with subsidiary matters. Clause 40.3 provides for imported manufactured articles to be dealt with outside the formula system by the use of a basic list and adjustment for invoiced prices, that is the system used in clause 39.3.

Clause 40.4 requires the relevant specialist formula to be used for sub-contractors. In the case of nominated sub-contractors, this appears out of place in the main contract and achieves nothing more than the exclusion provision of clause 39.6.2. In the case of domestic sub-contractors, the wording is not so strong as that of clause 39.4 and does not oblige the contractor to incorporate fluctuations provisions into the sub-contract: 'he shall, unless (they) . . . otherwise agree'. This reads strictly that he incorporates the provisions specified or none at all. The absence of provisions is not said to debar the contractor from any adjustment. Clause 40.4 is not at all satisfactory.

Clause 40.5 allows the quantity surveyor and the contractor to modify 'the methods and procedures for ascertaining the amount' and states that the result is final, so that arbitration is excluded. Under the first proviso given only a reasonable expectation of approximation to accuracy is required, leaving some leeway it seems. This is in relation to final adjustment: clause 40.6 deals with adjustments in the absence of monthly bulletins by requiring 'a fair and reasonable basis' to be used. Recalculation is to take place if the bulletins reappear in time and the interim method of calculation is to run as close as is practicable to the standard system, so as to ease this recalculation. The issue of the final certificate is not to be delayed on this score and if necessary is to be based on the fair and reasonable amounts. These are not therefore to be calculated as though they are just payments on account of a final statement: they may be the final amounts.

If the contractor is late in completing the works, clause 40.7 gives a similar effect to clause 39.5.7, even though it is rather differently phrased.

Chapter 10

INTERIM PAYMENTS AND FINAL SETTLEMENT

GENERAL CONSIDERATIONS

The title of this chapter indicates the major progression which runs through the elements of the contract considered here. Several earlier chapters touch upon how adjustments to the contract sum might occur and be dealt with, and such matters are the sole concern of that immediately preceding. This chapter considers the procedures for paying the contractor during and after construction, rather than the causes and calculations, and also the associated question of expressing final satisfaction with the works and, if necessary, settling any disputes. But while this progression is dominant, there are other themes, in particular matters of ownership of and responsibility for what is not fixed to the employer's land. Clause 30 does not deal with all certificates under the contract despite the generality of its title, but only with those used for payment and for expressing final satisfaction.

Clause 30 about certificates and payments is taken here as primary, while clause 16 about materials on and off-site and parts of clause 35 are brought in where arising out of clause 30. The subject-matter of clause 30 is itself arranged into six main themes for comment after the Synopsis. These themes are related to several underlying principles:

(a) There is a modification of the 'entire contract' principle (see Ch. 1) of paying the whole price at completion, with none of it before or after. This involves a regular pattern of payments on account before completion and a less regular pattern later, authorised by interim certificates. A proportion of the gross amount is held back as retention, with release of half at completion and the rest after defects have been made good. Interim payments may continue past this latter date, as progressive finalisation of the account throws up any sums, while the final balance is settled (in either direction) when the final certificate is issued. If there is partial possession or sectional completion (see Ch. 7 and example in Ch. 15), the timetable of retention reduction and the defects period are advanced for the parts concerned within the framework, while the final certificate remains as one for the whole of the works.

(*b*) The adjustments to the contract sum are given, with authority to include them in the interim payments as well as the final account.

(*c*) The method of valuing work for inclusion in interim certificates is not made explicit. It may be inferred to be by using quantities and prices from the contract bills and the related values of adjustments of the contract sum, in appropriate proportions. This is what is usually done in practice, although discretion is exercised over elements like preliminaries and work which may be of limited value until other work is performed, such as excavations when work is still to be constructed within them. There is also a recognised level of approximation, as is reasonable when the figures are only interim; work is being carried out daily and there is retention in hand.

(*d*) Not only work executed, but also unfixed materials may be included in interim payments. This is mandatory over materials on site, but optional and dependent upon a number of provisos over materials not yet on site. Payment for either category of materials raises questions of title and ownership. When once they are fixed in the works and so to the employer's land, they undoubtedly belong to him whether he has paid for them or not. The intention of the contract is that they become the property of the employer so soon as he pays for them, even though they are unfixed and may not even be on site. Looked at from the standpoint of the contract, this is laudable enough. The problem is that, in general, the contractor cannot pass on a better title than he himself possesses. If he has not paid for the materials when he is paid (a very common state of affairs), he may possess an inadequate title, depending upon the nature of the material and the terms of the contract of sale. Provided the works are then completed, or at least the materials are fixed, no problem arises. But in the event of the contractor's insolvency and determination of his employment at the wrong moment, serious problems may arise for the employer despite the provisions of the contract. Suppliers naturally view matters quite otherwise.

(*e*) The special position of nominated sub-contractors (rather than nominated suppliers) under the contract comes out in the degree of protection offered to them alone over payments, both interim and final. The contractor must demonstrate that he has made payments as directed and, in default of this, the employer may or even in some cases must, make the payments and recover from the contractor. All accounts of nominated sub-contractors are to be included sufficiently ahead of the final certificate to enable proof of payment to be produced by the contractor.

(*f*) The employer may hold a percentage of the gross value as retention, to give him some protection against defects and failure to complete in particular. This is counterbalanced by the establishment of a trust fund status for the retention, so that it is not lost in the event of the employer's insolvency. This arrangement is refined by the division of retention into separate parts for the contractor and for nominated sub-contractors, again emphasising the special position of the latter.

(g) The final certificate alone out of the certificates issued by the architect is given final effects on matters of satisfaction with the works and of finance. So far as the former goes, the effect is limited to matters of the architect's reasonable satisfaction, as is discussed hereafter. If therefore the employer is dissatisfied on these matters, his recourse is against the architect, but on all other questions of quality etc. he has the standard contractual remedies against the contractor within the period of limitation. On finance, the effect is more sweeping so that there is less scope for the employer to act against the contractor, but a correspondingly greater scope for raising matters of professional negligence. The finality of the final certificate is also made subject to arbitration and legal action within fairly narrow limits (see Ch. 15). As a corollary to the finality of this certificate other certificates are *not* final, although errors in them may well lead to a right of action or to other redress.

SYNOPSIS OF CLAUSES 16, 30

See Chapter 5 for synopsis of clause 35, parts of which are taken in the comments in this chapter.

CLAUSE 16: MATERIALS AND GOODS UNFIXED OR OFF-SITE

16.1 • Materials and goods on site, generally
   • not to be removed without architect's consent
   • to become property of employer
      • when paid for under interim certificate
      • but contractor still responsible for them

16.2 • Materials and goods off-site, when paid for under interim certificate
   • to become property of employer
   • not to be removed, except to works
   • but contractor
      • still responsible for them
      • to meet all costs until delivered to works

CLAUSE 30: CERTIFICATES

30.1 • Architect to issue certificates stating amounts due to contractor
  • employer to honour in 14 days
  • Employer may deduct from monies due, including retention paid over
    • if has right under contract
    • despite fiduciary interest in retention
    • must inform contractor of reason
  • Interim valuations to be made when necessary
    • (when clause 40 applies this amended)
  • Timing of interim certificates
    • regular at intervals given
      • until end of period including practical completion
    • occasional thereafter (minimum monthly)
      • when further amounts known
      • when retention to be reduced, after clearing defects

30.2 • Amount due in interim certificate to be
  • gross valuation (as defined below) to 7 days before certificate
  • less
    • retention
    • previous amounts
  • Valuation to include, subject to retention
    • work executed, with any clause 40 adjustments for fluctuations
    • materials
      • properly on site
      • specially allowed off-site
    • nominated sub-contract amounts and profit
  • Valuation to include, but not subject to retention
    • amounts for fees, setting out, opening up and testing, royalties, making good defects and special insurance
    • amounts for loss and expense
    • final payments to nominated sub-contractors
    • fluctuations additions calculated other than by formula
    • similar amounts for nominated sub-contractors
  • Valuation to allow deduction, but not subject to retention
    • fluctuations omissions calculated other than by formula
    • similar amounts for nominated sub-contractors

30.3 • Valuation may include materials off-site, at architect's discretion, provided
  • materials
    • intended for works

- completely prepared
- set apart and labelled adequately
- contract for supply to contractor written and provides for property in materials to pass to contractor by time prepared and set apart
- materials in accordance with contract
- contractor demonstrates
  - foregoing are so
  - materials insured until delivered to works

30.4 • Retention, rules for ascertainment
  - retention percentage to be 5% (unless appendix gives less) of relevant amounts in interim certificates
  - retention percentage may be deducted before practical completion
  - half retention percentage may be deducted between practical completion and certificate of making good defects
- Retention, distinguished as
  - contractor's retention
  - nominated sub-contract retention

30.5 • Retention, rules for treatment
  - employer's interest fiduciary, but need not invest
  - architect or quantity surveyor to prepare statement of all retention amounts with each interim certificate
  - statement to be issued to employer, contractor and each nominated sub-contractor concerned
  - employer to place retention in separate bank account
    - if required by contractor or *any* nominated sub-contractor
    - and certify so done
    - but may retain interest
  - if employer deducts amounts from retention, as allowed by contract, to notify contractor

30.6 • Procedure for final adjustment of contract sum
  - contractor to send all documents (included nominated) to architect or quantity surveyor
    - at latest, at reasonable time after practical completion
  - quantity surveyor then to prepare variation account within period stated in appendix
  - architect to send to contractor, with extract to each nominated sub-contractor
- Deduction adjustments to contract sum
  - prime cost sums etc. and profit
  - provisional sums etc.

- variation omissions
- fluctuations omissions
- any other amount under contract
- Addition adjustments to contract sum
  - nominated sub-contract accounts
  - contractor's accounts for nominated work performed
  - nominated supply accounts
  - profit on foregoing
  - amounts for fees, opening up and testing, royalties, making good defects and special insurance
  - variation additions
  - provisional sum work additions
  - amounts for loss and expense
  - insurance by contractor on employer's default
  - fluctuations additions
  - any other amount under contract
- Contractor to receive copy of computation of adjusted contract sum, before issue of final certificate

30.7
- Interim certificate to be issued to include final nominated sub-contract amounts
  - as soon as practicable
  - not later than 28 days before final certificate
  - not necessarily at least one month after previous interim certificate

30.8
- Final certificate to be issued and each nominated sub-contractor notified of date
  - before end of period stated in appendix following latest of
    - end of defects liability period
    - completion of making good defects
    - contractor sending documents for adjustment of contract sum to architect or quantity surveyor
  - to state
    - amounts stated in interim certificates
    - contract sum as adjusted
  - difference payable by one party to other in 14 days
    - without prejudice to outstanding interim certificates
    - subject to any deductions under contract

30.9
- Effect of final certificate
  - in arbitration or other proceedings, conclusive evidence
    - quality where to reasonable satisfaction of architect
    - adjustments of contract sum being made, except for accident or error
  - except where fraud
  - if arbitration etc. commenced before final certificate

- then final certificate conclusive after
  - conclusion of same and subject to results
  - 12 months inaction by parties and subject to any partial settlement
- if arbitration etc. commenced within 14 days of final certificate
  - final certificate conclusive
  - except on subject of arbitration etc.

30.10 • No certificate other than final certificate conclusive

COMMENTS ON CLAUSES 16, 30, 35.13, 35.17–35.19

For the reasons given at the beginning of the chapter, clause 30 is covered here under six main themes with clause 16 and the parts of clause 35 introduced when appropriate.

The timetable

It bears repeating that the architect is not required to express final, or indeed any, satisfaction with the contractor's work during progress (see Chs. 1 and 3). Most of the certificates under clause 30 are therefore limited to matters of payment, although obviously payment is only made on the basis that satisfactory work is thought to have been performed.

Interim certificates are governed by clause 30.1 and the architect is obliged by clause 30.1.1.1 to issue them at particular junctures (unless the contractor is prepared to be paid less often!) and the employer in turn to honour them by paying the contractor within fourteen days. No minimum amount for a certificate is prescribed by the clause, so that interim certificates must be issued when the conditions are fulfilled. During progress, certificates are due at regular intervals, which are usually stated in the appendix as a calendar month. Unless the appendix is more specific, the intervals are reckoned from when the work commences. This pattern carries over to the interim certificate following practical completion, so that the main reduction of retention at that time may be made. After this, the need for payments is not governed by the progress of the works but by the progress of financial settlement revealing balances outstanding, so that the irregular issue of certificates at minimum intervals of one month occurs. There is still no minimum amount, although it may be agreed to wait a while to gather up several amounts into a reasonable parcel.

Two subsidiary points arise. There is an unexplained reference in clause 30.2 to stage payments to which the parties may agree. This appears to relate to fixed values for fixed stages of the work, but without any change in the spacing of interim certificates. As such stages modify the contract intention about amounts of payments, the parties might however wish to use them to modify the timing as well. Secondly, the use of the alternative of formula fluctuations under clause 40 requires interim valuations to relate to a particular time of the month, so that this option reasonably also conditions the timing of the resultant interim certificates.

The reduction of retention (see example in Ch. 15) leads in itself to interim certificates, even though no further work has been done and no gross payments have been discovered. In the simplest case there are two reductions: the first half in the certificate following practical completion already mentioned, and the second in a certificate following the making good of defects. This is the effect of clause 30.4.1 discussed under the theme of 'Safeguards'. If however sectional completion or partial possession of a part of the work occurs (see Ch. 6), earlier reductions take place in respect of such a part. If there are several of these events, the pattern of retention reduction may become quite complex, with work changing financial status at a number of intervals.

A further disturbance occurs if *any* nominated sub-contractor is finally paid his retention and balance alike early, by the operation of clause 35.17. This is discussed later in this chapter and is distinct from the requirement of clause 30.7 that *all* nominated sub-contractors are to be paid off at least twenty-eight days before the issue of the final certificate. Only in the case of clause 30.7 may the certificate be issued closer than one month to that preceding it, so that issue of the final certificate is not delayed. In all the other cases the certificates must be at the normal intervals.

The final certificate clears any remaining balance and its wider effect is discussed under the theme of 'Settlement'. It is to be issued in accordance with clause 30.8 within a period given in the appendix and calculated from the latest of the three times given. There is distinct disadvantage to the employer and possible repercussions to the architect in issuing the schedule of defects, and so perhaps having them cleared, before the end of the defects liability period. On the other hand, it is often delays in obtaining information for the final certificate from the contractor that make the last of the three times the real signal. This event is often hard to identify, because information may come to hand in small pieces, and even when it has occurred delays in confirmation of instructions and agreeing amounts may extend affairs well beyond the contract intention.

Interim calculations
The duty of performing calculations for what is usually termed 'the

final account' to back up the final certificate is clearly laid on the quantity surveyor by clause 30.6.1. In the case of interim certificates, interim valuations are prepared by the quantity surveyor when the architect so deems fit under clause 30.1.2. If he wishes, the architect may otherwise make the calculations how he will. Interim valuations will almost invariably be prepared by the quantity surveyor. If formula fluctuations under clause 40 are applicable, valuations become obligatory under the amendment introduced there to clause 30.1.2.

While the method of calculation of the figures presented in certificates is not given, the elements which may be included are listed quite fully. In the case of interim certificates, this is the burden of clause 30.2 which divides into four sections. The introductory part sets out the principle of gross valuation less retention, and then of the deduction of 'the total amount stated as due' in all previous interim certificates, if any. The result here is an 'amount stated as due' in a particular certificate and this amount, and no less, should be calculated in any quantity surveyor's valuation. It should then be embodied in the architect's certificate, unless the architect wishes to exclude the value of any work etc. included by the quantity surveyor because it is not in accordance with the contract. Preferably though the architect should notify the quantity surveyor about this in advance, while the quantity surveyor should mention any doubtful work so that the architect has warning if he wishes to exclude it. There are other deductions that arise under the conditions: these are considered later in this section. The limitation on what must be included in a certificate to what is there seven days before the certificate (but not the valuation), takes account of the time-lag between the two documents. Later work and deliveries can be included, if necessary with last-minute verification.

The items which must be included in interim certificates are essentially straightforward. Work and materials delivered to site are the main constituents, covering the contributions of the contractor and all categories of suppliers and sub-contractors. Retention is deducted from all of these amounts under clause 30.2.1. It is necessary to identify the amounts for nominated sub-contractors in certificates to comply with clause 35.13.1, which requires the architect to direct the contractor on what is to be paid to them and to notify the sub-contractors of the amounts. It is also necessary to identify the amounts of retention on nominated sub-contractors, so that these amounts may be notified to them. This reflects the special treatment of nominated sub-contractors and is particularly needed if the architect is to check later whether payments have been made, as clause 35.13.3 requires of him and as is discussed under 'Safeguards for nominated sub-contractors'.

In the case of the contractor's work, which includes that of domestic sub-contractors, variations under clause 13.5 are to be subject to retention. The authority to include the value of them and other adjustments of the contract sum in interim certificates is given by clause 3. The other adjustments to the contract sum are listed as additions in clause 30.2.2 and as deductions in clause 30.2.3, and in both cases as *not* subject to retention and therefore as gross amounts. As these adjustments do not result directly from changes in what the employer is to receive under the contract and so do not represent the 'value' of what may yet prove to be defective, this arrangement is reasonable. Accordingly, the two lists include fluctuations calculations under two of the alternative clauses, clauses 38 and 39, where a direct analysis of labour returns and invoices is required. The third alternative of calculation by formula under clause 40 is given in clause 30.2.1.1, so that in this case retention is deducted. This is inconsistent in principle, but takes practical account of the method of calculation, which in that case is directly dependent on adjustment of measured work values.

While all of these items *must* be included, clause 30.2.1.3 refers to other materials which the architect *may* include 'in the exercise of his discretion under clause 30.3'. That clause refers to materials 'before delivery'. Unless there is any prior statement in the contract bills that the clause will be operated for particular materials, it is entirely optional. Otherwise, even when the contractor demonstrates that he can meet all of its requirements, the architect need not include the value of such materials. If he does wish to include the value, and this will clearly ease the contractor's financial burden, he must ensure that every one of the nine provisos that is relevant is met. In summary these relate to physical condition, in terms of specification, fabrication and identification, and to commercial status, in terms of legal title and insurance.

What must *not* be done in calculating the amount stated as due in an interim certificate is to take any account of sums which the employer is allowed by the conditions to deduct from payments. These sums are listed in Chapter 15 and in essence are due to a failure by the contractor to discharge an obligation to perform work or pay others. Of these sums, those due to non-payment of nominated sub-contractors present the most complications and are discussed under 'Safeguards for nominated sub-contractors'. The principle is that the architect certifies what is due as if no contra-amounts have arisen and that then the employer exercises his discretion or obligation, as the case may be, to deduct these amounts. The amounts are not adjustments to the contract sum, as they are not the result of authorised activities of the contractor.

This same principle carries through to the final certificate considered below and so the amount should not be deducted in that certificate either.

When certificates following one from which a deduction has been made are issued, it is necessary to follow the clause strictly and deduct 'the total amount stated as due in Interim Certificates previously issued'. This means the unreduced previous amounts. If the previous amounts are reduced and then deducted from any current gross valuation, the result is to increase the amount of that current payment and so pass to the contractor what has previously been withheld. This is illustrated in Chapter 15.

Final calculations

With clause 30.6 matters move to final adjustment of the contract sum in preparation for the issue of the final certificate. Clause 30.6.1 covers two preliminary exchanges of information. There are sub-contract accounts, invoices, daywork sheets, fluctuations details and so forth that only the contractor can produce for the quantity surveyor to work on. Many of these data will be forthcoming during progress, but otherwise the 'reasonable time' provision comes into play. If the contractor does not produce them, he is delaying the settlement which he desires. The other part of the exchange is the statement of valuations under clause 13, that is the priced account of variations and the expenditure of provisional sums, which it is the quantity surveyor's duty to prepare. In places this account will depend on the contractor's information, such as invoices for pricing and daywork details. This exchange enables the contractor to check what he is to receive against the 'notes' that he may have taken under clause 13.6 and helps the quantity surveyor to gather everything together into one document, which is usually termed 'the final account'. In practice the preparation of this account proceeds from the early days of the contract, with much relatively piecemeal exchange of information from time to time.

More particularly, the accounts for nominated sub-contractors are usually prepared as subsidiary entities between them and the quantity surveyor rather than dispersed about the main account as the clause portrays. The thrust of the clause here is that the contractor is entitled to be involved in the settlement of all accounts, partly because of his profit element, more materially perhaps to debate whether some sub-contractor charges are to be met by the employer in the final account or by the contractor himself outside the account.

Clause 30.6.2 lists the deduction and addition elements of adjustment which come into the final account, some of these corresponding explicitly to the elements for interim payment listed in clause 30.2. They are all covered by the general authority to adjust in clause 3 and specific references in other clauses, most of which are given by number in clause 30.6.2. Most of these therefore need no comment beyond what is given elsewhere. Along with provisional sums, there is a reference to 'work described as provisional', which work is not mentioned in clause 13 but which leads to no extra problem for that reason. It is omitted in its entirety and the actual work added in its place. Both the deduction and addition lists end with 'any other amount . . . required'. The amounts permissible here appear to be only renomination expenses over sub-contractors and special expenses in connection with nominated suppliers.

The amount of the final account goes forward into the final certificate to give 'the Contract Sum adjusted as necessary' under clause 30.8.2. There is no direct requirement for the quantity surveyor and contractor to have reached agreement on this amount or on any of the contents of the account. The quantity surveyor is to allow the contractor to take notes of variation and other measurements under clause 13.6, so that the contractor is not denied information. The quantity surveyor is then to supply to the contractor a priced account under clause 30.6.1 covering measured work and daywork within the period of final measurement, provided he has had information from the contractor in time.

Lastly, the quantity surveyor is to supply the contractor with a copy of the whole account under clause 30.6.3 at an undefined time before the issue of the final certificate. Usually exchange of information and agreement of parts of the account will be closely linked, even if some agreement remains provisional until the whole picture of the account emerges. At worst, the contractor has fourteen days from the issue of the certificate to seek arbitration on its content and this may be on the amount stated in it. The contractor must however be explicit here and this may be more than difficult if the account under clause 30.6.3 has only reached him the day before! This is unreasonable, even if it is the letter of the contract. More reasonably, if the quantity surveyor cannot obtain advance agreement within a sensible time from the contractor, he may recommend to the architect that the final certificate should include the unagreed figure and so force the contractor's hand one way or the other.

There is no requirement for either the employer or the architect to agree the account or even, strictly, to see it. It may be prudent to warn the employer what is coming, as he otherwise may have a surprise and only fourteen days to seek arbitration, with again the need on his part to be explicit about where his objection lies when, even more than the contractor, he lacks the detail to tell. While the architect has to authorise in principle what goes into the account by way of variation instructions etc. and while he may review nominated sub-contract accounts etc. as they pass through his hands, he cannot determine the details of settlement. The only exception occurs if he retains for himself the ascertainment of loss and expense amounts. He usually does not, both on grounds of the expertise required and of the overlap of amounts with the main stream reimbursement.

Safeguards for employer

Clause 30 and also clause 35 contain provisions that afford some protection on two matters. Particularly obvious is the establishment of a retention fund to give a financial reserve for the employer. Under clause 30.4.1, the full amount of 5 per cent (unless modified) is held back from the value of those elements listed in clause 30.2.1 until practical completion is achieved. This is an incentive to the contractor to complete and some cushion if he fails to complete, especially if he is insolvent. After practical completion the percentage retained is halved until defects are cleared. Whether the fund held is always sufficient protection in these cases is not for discussion here; when insolvency occurs it often is not.

Retention is intended eventually to pass to the contractor, and so it is declared by clause 30.5.1 that the employer has purely a trustee interest. This is a good intention that may come to nothing if the employer becomes insolvent and the fund cannot be identified in the aftermath. Clause 30.5.3 therefore allows the contractor or any nominated sub-contractor to request a separate account to be maintained for the retention. It would appear literally that even the nominated sub-contractor with the smallest interest can have the *whole* of the retention so treated. The statement of clause 30.5.2 acts to identify how much is due to whom in the funds. This arrangement does not prevent the employer deducting from the retention monies if current payments otherwise due do not provide enough for his proper needs. Clause 30.1.1 allows him to deduct, but he must notify the contractor under clause 30.5.4.

The second major area is the value of materials. These are to be included as of right if on site and at the architect's discretion otherwise. For materials on site, the only stipulations in clause 30.2.1 are that they are not to be on site too early and that they are to be properly protected. The former needs a balance to be struck: the employer should not have to pay too early and so be outstanding on his money, but if the contractor obtains materials later there may be more for the employer to pay in fluctuations increases. The latter is important if weather damage or theft is likely. The value of anything so lost will be taken out in the next certificate, but meantime there is effectively less retention available. For materials off-site the same considerations apply, but they are often overshadowed by questions of ownership. Here the requirements of clause 30.3 already discussed are intended to, and usually do, give adequate protection of the employer's interests.

It is the case however, as mentioned under (d) at the beginning of this chapter, even with materials on site, that problems crop up over title if the employer pays for what the contractor does not own. Clause 16 about unfixed materials attempts to help here by declaring that the title passes with payment, for both categories of materials, but this does nothing if the contractor has no title. Provided there is a good title, it is helpful by forbidding the removal of materials except to site. When they are on site this applies whether they are paid for or not, but if they are still off-site it is contingent upon payment being made. Clause 16.2 also makes the contractor responsible for insurance and transport costs, until the general responsibilities of clause 16.1 are assumed on delivery.

Safeguards for nominated sub-contractors
A number of safeguards over payments are included in the conditions on behalf of nominated sub-contractors. The identification of amounts for these persons under clause 30.2.1 and of retention held on their work and materials under clause 30.4 has already been mentioned. Clause 35 contains some further provisions to give protection to them over payments which, because they *are* sub-contractors, are made to them through the contractor. The procedure and stipulation over payments in general are given in clause 35.13 and extra matters about final payments in particular in clauses 35.17–35.19.

It is the architect's standing responsibility under clause 35.13.1 to control payments to nominated sub-contractors by including particular amounts in any interim certificate and directing the contractor to pay these amounts. These are interim or final amounts after deduction of any retention and, subject to this deduction, the contractor must pay them and neither more nor less to meet clause 35.13.2. (The reference only to 'interim' appears to be an error and, if not deleted, makes the rest of the clause ineffective over final amounts.) The architect, who will usually be advised by the quantity surveyor, has the duty of advising each nominated sub-contractor of these amounts. The only case in which the contractor may pass less is one falling within the set-off provisions of sub-contract clause 23, which allow properly authenticated contra-amounts to be deducted.

Before issuing the next interim certificate, the architect must perform several actions under clause 35.13.4 and the first part of clause 35.13.5. He is to seek proof that the amount in the previous certificate for each nominated sub-contractor has been passed on; often the quantity surveyor will do this as a sub-routine of preparing the supporting valuation. If proof is lacking, the architect can pass it over only if the lapse is on the part of the sub-contractor in providing it. Otherwise he must certify to the employer the amount of the deficiency. He must not however reduce the next interim certificate to take any account of this amount, as already pointed out.

Upon receipt of the architect's special certificate and if neither of Agreements NSC/2 or NSC/2a is in force, the employer has a choice whether or not to make a direct payment to the sub-contractor. If an agreement is in force he is obliged to do this, under the terms of the agreement. He is to make it at the same time as he pays the contractor under the next interim certificate and he is to reduce that amount by the same sum. In issuing the following interim certificate, the architect must again make no deduction of this sum, which falls into the category of deductions mentioned under 'Interim calculations', to avoid refunding it to the contractor (see example in Ch. 15).

Several stipulations are given in clause 35.13.5. The employer is not obliged to pay out more than he has available, which is the net amount of the next interim certificate. If that certificate includes some reduction of retention to be paid over to another nominated sub-contractor, even that amount is not available because of its trust status and must go to that other person. If more than one nominated sub-contractor is eligible for direct payment and the amount available is inadequate, then it is to be shared out in proportion or according to some reasonable criterion, such as who has been waiting longest. The whole process of direct payment must come to an immediate halt if the contractor passes into insolvency.

Two points follow from these arrangements. There is not only no obligation on the employer to pay an amount direct in the first place rather than through an interim certificate, because it is feared that the contractor will not pass it on, but it is not permissible for the employer to do this. He can act only over an amount on which there has been a default. Also if an interim certificate includes amounts other than retention for nominated sub-contractors, these *are* available to form part of the current fund for direct payments (see further example in Ch. 15).

The provisions for final payment of nominated sub-contractors in clause 35.17 are to be read in the context of the foregoing. They allow early complete paying-off of a nominated sub-contractor through an interim certificate when Agreement NSC/2 or NSC/2a is in force and unamended in certain clauses, but not otherwise. This is to be done within the twelve-month period following completion of the sub-contract work. It may be overtaken, whether a collateral agreement is in force or not, by the provision of clause 30.7 for all nominated sub-contractors to be paid off at least twenty-eight days before the final certificate and if necessary out of sequence with the ordinary rhythm of interim certificates. These arrangements not only secure early payment, they may actually secure payment, because if the contractor defaults the employer can pay direct. This is subject to the availability of an adequate balance due in the final certificate to permit all direct payments.

Payment under clause 35.17 is conditional upon the provisos given. They will have already been met before clause 30.7 comes into use. However when clause 35.17 is operated, it is necessary to protect the contractor against any residual liabilities before he is paid off (but not cleared of all liability) under the final certificate, so that there is still a specialist to do remedial work if the nominated sub-contractor fails. Clause 35.18 allows for a further nomination, but with the contractor carrying any cost that the employer cannot recover through the collateral agreement. This is conditional on the contractor agreeing in advance to the substituted price.

Clause 35.19 ensures that final payment of a nominated sub-contractor does not erode the contractor's overall liabilities for the works, and that insurance of the works is not reduced.

The final settlement

There are two major aspects here: finance and quality. Clause 30.8 covers the former of these and requires the final certificate to set out the difference between the total of interim certificates issued (even if not paid at the date of the final certificate) and the amount of the final account showing the adjusted contract sum. As always, none of these figures should take account of any deductions made or to be made by the employer. The figures stated are 'conclusive evidence' and can be reviewed only as clause 30.9 provides, that is if there is fraud, an accident or error in the calculations leading up to them or if they fall within any outstanding arbitration or legal action. The matter of error and so forth may be quite wide-ranging. It relates to the inclusion or omission of complete items, to an error in the computation of items that are included and to any error in price, extension or total. But also it relates back through the final account to the contract bills to take any uncorrected error in them, other than a pricing error which clause 14.2 excludes from adjustment.

Notification of the date of issue of the final certificate, but not its contents, is to be given to all nominated sub-contractors so that they are aware of when their residual liabilities at law will run out. There is no financial significance for them at this point.

It is not necessary for the final certificate to express any particular satisfaction over quality, since clause 30.9.1 gives its effect, subject again to fraud and outstanding proceedings. It is 'conclusive evidence' where quality is to be to the architect's 'reasonable satisfaction', so that wherever the contract documents and any instructions have used this expression, the contractor is relieved of liability by the issue of the certificate. Correspondingly, however, the architect assumes liability to the employer if a question of professional negligence arises, and so must check the works adequately before issuing the certificate. In most instances the standard of work and materials is expressed by reference to British Standards or other objective criteria, and here the contractor remains liable for any defect during the limitation period which runs from any breach on his part (see Ch. 1).

The final certificate is conclusive on the matters stated in any proceedings, so that it conditions those proceedings and an arbitrator or the courts cannot go behind it to reopen the matters so concluded. This is subject to the provisos in the latter part of clause 30.9, under which it is itself conditioned by two cases of proceedings. In clause 30.9.2 there is the case of proceedings begun before the issue of the final certificate. The architect may not delay issue simply because of unconcluded proceedings, as the certificate has a number of effects that must not be delayed, but is to issue the certificate which is then subject to the outcome of those proceedings or to any agreed terms by the time that the twelve month lapse occurs. It is not necessary to endorse the certificate to this effect, although a notification to the parties may avoid misunderstanding.

Alternatively the very issue of the final certificate may provoke proceedings. The architect exercises his own judgement in issuing the final certificate, and indeed must not allow himself to be influenced by either party, otherwise the certificate may be set aside as not proper. The availability of proceedings under clause 30.9.3 allows an aggrieved party to seek redress over what may therefore be a difference of opinion with the architect, even though the dispute will be conducted as against the other party. Such proceedings must be started within fourteen days of issue of the certificate, or the opportunity will be lost.

Proceedings in general and arbitration in particular are dealt with in Chapter 15.

CHAPTER 11

OTHER EDITIONS OF THE JCT CONTRACT AND THE SCOTTISH CONTRACTS

As mentioned in Chapter 2, there are six variants of the JCT standard form of building contract. These are of almost identical structure and very similar in content and differ only on account of their distinctive purposes. These are to allow for use by private clients or local authority clients and in each of these cases to provide three financial bases, these being (firm) quantities, approximate quantities and without quantities.

The differences produced by the various financial bases are more significant than those due to the two types of client, even though the latter produce a greater number of minor differences. It is possible therefore to cover the salient points of all five variant editions by comparing only three of them with the private edition with quantities treated in the preceding chapters. These are the other two private editions, approximate quantities and without quantities, and the local authorities edition with quantities. The points in the other two local authorities editions may be deduced from this approach.

This chapter ends with a section on the differences in Scottish documents referred to in Chapter 2.

OTHER JCT EDITIONS

The private edition with approximate quantities

All the fundamental differences in this edition are due to the nature of the quantities provided for tendering and incorporated into the contract and resulting matters of remeasurement and valuation. These differences may be traced through the clauses, leaving smaller points to be gathered up at the end.

A note at the beginning of this contract form, but not forming part of the contract, states that it is intended for use when the works have been 'substantially designed' and when the 'quantities . . . are approximate and subject to remeasurement'. These expressions should both be noted. The first limits intended use of the form to a situation of fairly advanced design, which is by no means the only instance in practice when approximate quantities may be pressed into service. The second declares the status of the quantities, but gives no indication of their degree of approximation. While they can be no more accurate than the drawings on which they are based, they could be considerably less.

The preambles of the articles of agreement take this point further as part of the contract by stating that there are 'Drawings and Bills of Approximate Quantities showing and describing, and intending to set out a reasonably accurate forecast of, the quantity of the work to be done', so that the quantities need to be quite a good indication to the contractor when tendering. But the expression also means that *both* drawings and bills forecast the quantity of work as well as describe the work in their respective ways. This is not the case under the 'with quantities' editions, where only the bills establish the quantities, and that on a firm basis. There the drawings may be referred to during tendering as showing the general nature of the works and may be taken into account in setting the level of pricing, but not the quantities themselves.

In the present case the arithmetical product of the quantities in the bills and the unit rates must still be used to arrive at the tender and not some adjustment of the quantities which the contractor assesses from the drawings. This is evident from clause 13 which here again gives the quality and *quantity* of work as those in the contract bills. But in arriving, for instance, at the figures for major items of plant and so at the prices into which these figures are incorporated, the contractor is invited by the wording given to take note of drawings *and* bills. It is therefore important that the two are in reasonable accord to avoid possible misunderstanding over which dominated the original calculation. Otherwise uncertainty will extend into the final valuation of the work as executed when an adjustment of unit rates to take account of shifts in the quantities from those in the contract bills may be needed.

Clause 14 is titled 'Measurement and valuation of work, including variations and provisional sums' and proceeds closely on the pattern of clause 13 in the 'with quantities' editions. In terms of instructions, it refers to 'modification of the design', rather than alteration of quantity, as all quantities are subject to remeasurement. The wording assumes the possibility of the architect working from the basis of the contract drawings and issuing variation drawings under this clause and supplementary drawings under clause 5.4. The practicability of doing this depends on how accurate and firm the contract drawings are. If they are being substantially changed or developed, it may be less complex simply to instruct that they be disregarded and that a complete fresh set be substituted. There is also the danger, when trying to modify the effect of drawings considerably, of ambiguities creeping in or gaps being left.

When it is clear what the contractor should do, the question of valuation is straightforward, subject to the comments already made about the basis of the contract pricing. There is to be remeasurement of all work 'in accordance with clause 2.1', that is the original contract work, and under 'instructions issued under clauses. 14.2 and 14.3', that is variations and expenditure of provisional sums. A complete summation is required of all work, rather than the 'additions and omissions' approach of the other edition. The pricing rules follow those of that edition, tempered by the change in quantity stipulation and again including the possibility of adjusting prices for essentially unvaried work if the omission of other work affects it.

Clause 30.6.2 consists of a single list of items to be aggregated to give what is termed the ascertained final sum, and so carries through the remeasurement policy in preparation for the final certificate. There are one or two minor differences between this and the 'with quantities' edition here, but they do not affect the practical outcome. In addition, clause 30.1.2 requires interim valuation for all interim certificates, as there are no firm quantities to be used as a guide on a proportioning basis.

Smaller consequences of the financial basis of this form may be listed:

(*a*) The employer's consideration in the articles of agreement is given as a 'sum or sums as shall become payable'.

(*b*) The contractor's responsibility to raise errors in the contract bills under clause 2.2.2.2 is limited to matters of description, as he cannot place reliance on the quantities.

(*c*) The architect may bring in others to perform work under clause 4.1.2, as in the other edition. If he does, the work must be measured as though the contractor has performed it and the actual cost then deducted in the final account.

(*d*) An additional relevant 'event' in clause 25 leading to extension of time is delay due to work differing in amount or character from what was forecast in the contract. There is however no right to loss and expense or determination by the contractor on this score under clauses 26 and 28.

(*e*) Clause 38 about limited fluctuations adjustment for statutory matters is omitted. In a contract with quite a measure of financial uncertainty, fluctuations adjustment is not to be restricted.

The private edition without quantities

In positive terms, this edition has the specification as the contract document in place of the contract bills in the 'with quantities' edition. The contractor therefore has to arrive at his tender by preparing any quantities that he may require by his own analysis of the contract drawings and specification, as a prelude to pricing such quantities as part of his tender. These quantities do not form part of the contract, which is based upon a simple lump sum, although there is provision for a schedule of rates for variations. The implication of this arrangement is that the contract is intended for fairly small works or, at most, moderately sized works of a simple nature. Despite this, the contract is as lengthy as the other editions and identical in comparable wording, even to the extent of the full clauses on nominated persons.

The contract drawings are those on which the contractor bases his tender, which becomes the contract sum usually without any adjustment. As there are no quantities provided, these contract drawings must include *all* the drawings right down to details on which the quantities would have been based, rather than just those drawings which show the character of the work. It is therefore disconcerting that clause 5.4 still allows the architect to issue 'further drawings and details . . . to explain and amplify the Contract Drawings'. These are *not* variation drawings and should already be with the contractor when he tenders.

The specification is the other technical document on which the contractor bases his tender. Most of the detail in it will correspond to what is in the preambles of the contract bills under the other editions. It must also contain any positional information and schedules to be read in conjunction with the contract drawings so that quantities can be deduced. This is unnecessary when the quantities are provided, in which case the detail can follow post-contractually under clause 5.3.

Clause 14.1 therefore gives the specification as describing, and the contract drawings as showing the quality and quantity of work in the contract, so that they must be read together. This is tidy, so long as there is no divergence between specification and drawings. If there is, the contractor is to seek an instruction from the architect under clause 2.3 about what work is actually to be performed, as in the other editions. Over financial aspects, the wording of clauses 2.2.2 and 14.1 over errors and omissions is more difficult. The former has 'any error in description or in quantity or omission of items' and the latter 'the quality and quantity of the work included in the Contract Sum', with the references in both cases to both drawings and specification. In the 'with quantities' editions, these terms refer to such defects within the contract bills alone as incorrect quantities or descriptions. As only the contract bills give the 'quantity of the work included in the Contract Sum' in those editions, financial adjustment follows quite clearly upon correction of any error or omission. In the present contract, there is no certainty over what is included in the contract sum if the drawings and specification clash, only if they both have the same error or omission. No rule can be laid down, since no priority of one document over the other is given here. Each case must be decided on any merits it possesses.

The schedule of rates is to be provided by the contractor under clause 5.3.1.3 if not 'previously so provided'. It is far better to agree it before entering into the contract, so that any queries can be solved before either party is committed. It should consist simply of a list of item descriptions with the unit of measurement and price per unit for each item. Clause 13.5 provides for it to be used as the basis for valuing variations in a similar way to the contract bills under other editions. It should therefore contain items for any work in the contract likely to be subjected to variation and also a set of daywork provisions. There is no requirement for the measured items to be based upon the SMM, although their underlying basis should be clear.

There are two common ways of obtaining the schedule of rates. One is to ask the contractor to insert rates into a blank schedule forwarded to him when tendering. This has the advantage of ensuring that the wording is clear and contractually tidy, but the possible disadvantage of the rates not being at the same level as the tender, which they do not affect in any way. Alternatively the contractor may be asked to supply the measured and priced build-up of his tender. From this may be deleted all quantities and extensions, so that only descriptions, units and rates remain: these being the constituents of a schedule of rates. This approach reverses the advantages and disadvantages of the other. In either case some negotiated adjustment of rates or wording may be desirable and it is quite in order, since these elements have not entered directly into the competition leading up to the contract sum itself.

Whatever is done to establish the schedule, no adjustment of the contract sum arises because of errors in either quantities or rates on the part of the contractor when tendering. This is the extended effect of clause 14.2 in this case. The only adjustment arising is that resulting from errors and omissions in the documents supplied to the contractor when tendering, that is the drawings and specification.

Bills of quantities are introduced in clause 14.3 rather unexpectedly in the light of the last paragraph. The possibility of supplying such documents to the contractor 'at any time' (although most likely when he is tendering) is mentioned, but these are then stated not to be part of the contract, explicitly over rates and implicitly over quantities. Any practice of supplying information on which the contractor may not rely is at best useless and at worst bad, and should not be followed. There is also a drafting error in clause 2.2.1 which mentions that the 'Contract Bills' shall not override the conditions etc. This should be amended to 'Specification', as the side-heading correctly has it.

Subsidiary points of comparison with the 'with quantities' editions may be listed:

(*a*) Although there are no contract quantities, the contract provides for the possibility of a quantity surveyor. If a separate person is not required, it is possible to insert the name of the architect in the articles of agreement and for him to perform the appropriate functions, as the title 'quantity surveyor' is not protected.

(*b*) Clause 19.3.1 refers in part to domestic sub-contract work as 'priced in the Schedule of Rates'. Unless the schedule of rates covers everything (as it need not), this strictly imposes a pointless limitation.

(*c*) Clause 35.1 defining nominated sub-contractors ends with the same reference as the other editions to the SMM. This is superfluous, but appears harmless in the context.

(*d*) Clause 40 for formula fluctuations is not included, as it cannot be used in the absence of a rigid breakdown of the contract sum and supporting quantities.

The local authorities edition with quantities
This edition has no really substantial differences from its private counterpart, although it differs in several places needing comment.

The articles of agreement introduce options.   The chief officer may or may not be a registered architect, so that alternative clauses are given and one must be deleted. In the body of the conditions he is referred to as 'Architect/Supervising Officer' and no alterations are needed there. For both architect and quantity surveyor the article about objecting to a successor is to be deleted if it is the authority's own officer. The attestation clause is left blank to suit the authority's own policy. While contracting under seal is not obligatory, it does introduce a valuable longer limitations period.

Two extra clauses are introduced.   Clause 19A 'Fair Wages' requires the contractor and his sub-contractors to observe the House of Commons Resolution and breach of this becomes a cause for the employer to determine under clause 27.1.4. There is also clause 27.3 giving corrupt acts by the contractor and his servants, but not his sub-contractors, as a cause for the employer to determine. It extends to very small matters, even when the contractor may not know of the act concerned, and to other contracts than the present.

Several omissions occur and may be grouped:

(*a*) Under clause 22B the employer assumes the risk of the clause 22 perils but is not required to insure, although he may choose to do so. Clause 22C *does* require him to insure, but gives the contractor no right to check on this or do anything about a failure to insure. (There is a resultant omission of clause 30.6.2.14 over reimbursing the contractor for any extra premiums.) A local authority may well wish to be its own insurer in the first instance, but this does not explain the inconsistency in the second.

(*b*) There is no clause 28.1.4 giving insolvency of the employer as grounds for determination and no clause 30.5.3 about setting up a separate trust account for retention monies. These reflect the putative stability of local government finances.

(*c*) Clause 30.8 drops the fixed margin of three months from the various events regulating the issue of the final certificate and refers to the appendix, where the three months reappears as applying in the absence of an insertion, which is not to exceed six months in any case. The possible increase here is presumably to allow for audit, delay in which does not justify the employer in failing to honour the final certificate when due.

Fluctuations clauses 38, 39 and 40 all occur in full. There is the addition for clause 40 formula fluctuations of a provision in clause 40.1.3 and in the appendix for a 'non-adjustable element', which is not to exceed 10 per cent. This means that the total of fluctuations is to be reduced by the given percentage, on grounds of increased productivity and so forth.

SCOTTISH BUILDING CONTRACTS

The reason for special forms in Scotland lies in differences of law and the result is the array of documents outlined in Chapter 2. Only the major forms need be referred to here to explain the substantial differences. These forms are:

(*a*) Each of the JCT main forms with and without quantities (but not with approximate quantities) and nominated sub-contract forms produced without articles of agreement and appendix, that is as 'conditions only' documents.

(*b*) A Scottish Building Contract consisting of the equivalent of the JCT articles of agreement and referring to and incorporating the JCT conditions and the Scottish Supplement. This is followed by the Scottish Supplement itself which consists of two appendices respectively amending clauses in the JCT conditions and providing the equivalent of the JCT appendix. This may be used with any of the four sets of JCT conditions mentioned in (*a*). A second version of the contract contains a variant first appendix which is expanded to take in the further amendments to produce a sectional completion contract, thus replacing the JCT Supplement.

(*c*) A Scottish Building Sub-Contract arranged in a similar way to the main contract.

(*d*) Two 'Contracts relative to the purchase of materials and/or goods', one between employer and contractor and the other between employer, contractor and sub-contractor (nominated or domestic).

Several significant points needing brief mention arise from these documents, as well as a number of incidental drafting changes. The contract establishes the law of Scotland as applying to arbitrations and to the contract itself. The normal provision is for signing as sealing does not apply in Scotland, although the benefits of sealing may be secured by other means. There are also a number of changes to reflect the different law over insolvency, although the effect is very similar.

The possibility of insolvency lies behind the most important practical change. This is needed because JCT clauses 16.2 and 30.3 are not valid under Scotland's law. These clauses are therefore deleted and a different clause 30.3 only is introduced which allows the employer the option of entering into a separate direct contract of purchase so that ownership of materials off-site will pass to him. The value of the materials is then deducted from the contract and the employer pays 95 per cent of the value direct immediately and the rest when final reduction of retention occurs. Other clauses of the contract over such elements as damage and insurance still apply to the materials in question.

There are two versions of the contract of purchase. One is simply between employer and contractor and is used when the contractor owns the material himself immediately before the employer purchases them. The other is used when a sub-contractor owns the materials and is primarily between him and the employer. It is necessary for the contractor to sign as well, to give consent to the purchase and to maintain his liabilities. Instructions attached to the two contracts are similar to most of the provisions of JCT clause 30.3 to be observed when paying for materials off-site.

CONTRACT THEMES

CHAPTER 12

AN EXPLANATION AND SUMMARIES

The introduction to this book explains the differences in approach between Parts 2 and 3. This chapter begins with further explanation on using Part 3 and then sets out two sections which link Parts 2 and 3.

Chapters 13–15 are structured as a series of contract main themes and subsidiary themes. Each chapter deals with a group of themes and between them they cover the more important aspects of the JCT forms. There is quite an amount of overlap and therefore repetition between the themes, although the level of detail varies according to the context. Under each subsidiary theme, the material is presented in tabulated form and, where applicable, contract clause references are given alongside individual points. Cross-references between themes and to chapters in Part 2 have been employed sparingly. Instead the second section of this present chapter lists all the main and subsidiary themes in the following chapters, so that their structure may be grasped quickly and separated themes may be linked and compared.

This arrangement gives several levels of detail for a general study of the subject-matter of the contract or for preparation to take examinations. It also provides a classified index to the clauses themselves and so to the discussions in Part 2.

The other section of this chapter consists of summaries of Chapters 3–10 of Part 2. These summaries cover the 'General considerations' and 'Comments' sections of the chapters, but obviously not the 'Synopses'. Usually they give the sub-divisions used explicitly or otherwise an analysis in the order of writing, but this order is not slavishly followed. The summaries may be used to review the contents of the chapters when these have been read, as an outline for the reader's own notes and as a sequential index to the chapters to aid linking between chapters. Alongside the points listed, references to themes in Part 3 have been given in somewhat variable intensity. These are prefixed by chapter numbers so that they may be found directly or via the latter section of this chapter.

SUMMARIES OF CHAPTERS IN PART 2

See the beginning of this chapter for the way in which these lists
may be used. Chapter 11 in Part 2 has not been summarised, as
its own contents are by way of summary and comparison.

Chapter 3: Scope and carrying out of the works
(*Clauses 1–12, 14*)   *Part 3 ref.*

GENERAL CONSIDERATIONS

	13. Persons and organisations
• Architect's responsibilities	13. Architect
	14. Scope of works
• Contractor's responsibilities	13. Contractor
	14. Works and site
	14. Indemnity, injury and insurance
• Information communication	14. Documents
• Architect's verification	13. Design and quality
• Contract sum adjustment	15. Contract sum and adjustment

COMMENTS ON CLAUSES

• Documents and information	
• contract drawings	14. Contract documents
• contract bills	
• discrepancies	
• post-contract information	14. Post-contract documents
• Contractor's actions	
• construction of works	13. Performance obligations
• conforming to conditions,	13. Contract rights
quality and statute	
• master programme	
• person-in-charge	
• Architect's actions	13. Architect, in general
• supplying information	
• issuing and confirming instructions	
• quality maintenance	
• inspection and access	
• clerk of works	
• certificates	
• Financial matters	15. Contract sum and adjustment
• contract sum	
• adjustments	
• royalties	

Chapter 4: Other persons working on the site
(*Clauses 19, 29*)

GENERAL CONSIDERATIONS
- Modification of right of possession
  - sub-letting
  - nomination
  - direct contracts
  - public bodies
- Methods
  - defining types
  - introduction
  - operation
- Reasons for use of patterns

13. Contractor, contract rights
13. Architect, other persons working
13. Sub-contractors and suppliers
13. Sub-contractors and suppliers, procedures for appointment

COMMENTS ON CLAUSES
- Sub-letting, two ways of introducing
- Direct contracts, two ways of introducing

Chapter 5: Nomination of sub-contractors and suppliers
(*Clauses 35, 36*)

GENERAL CONSIDERATIONS
- Nomination
  - principles
  - reasons
  - special position created
- Basic and alternative methods and documents
- Nomination procedures
  - preparatory actions
  - nomination
  - progress actions
- Nominated sub-contract tender
- Employer/nominated sub-contractor agreement
- Simplifications over nominated suppliers
- Nominated supplier form of tender and warranty

13. Sub-contractors and suppliers, in general

COMMENTS ON CLAUSES

- Nomination of sub-contractors
  - definitions and identification
  - relation to employer agreement
  - procedure
    - basic method, defined with employer agreement
    - alternative method, undefined with agreement optional
    - change of method
    - problems of lapse, objection
  - renomination, causes and actions
- Nomination of suppliers
  - procedures
  - accounts for supply
  - contract of sale

13. Sub-contractors and suppliers, in general

Chapter 6: Progress of the works
(Clauses 17, 18, 23–25)

GENERAL CONSIDERATIONS

- Defined contract period and regular progress
- Results of late possession and completion
- Extension of time avoids liquidated damages
- No overall acceleration may be instructed
- Possible link of extension with loss and damage
- Practical completion
  - ends instructing new work
  - starts defects liability period
- Phased completion by
  - sectional completion

13. Contractor, performance obligations and contract rights.

- partial possession
- Phased commencement not provided
- Contractor's own programme in between, with no limitation over discretionary
  - early completion
  - acceleration in mid-progress

COMMENTS ON CLAUSES

• Normal progress and postponement	13. Architect, progress
	14. Execution of works
	14. Site of works
• Damages for non-completion	14. Progress and disturbance
• Interim extension of time	
• three stages of contractor's actions	
• architect's actions	
• Final extension of time	
• Mitigation of delay, co-operation by contractor	
• Nominated sub-contractors	
• Relevant events	14. Causes of delay
• Practical completion and making good defects	
• Partial early possession	

Chapter 7: Disturbance of progress of the works
(*Clauses 26–28, 32–34*)

GENERAL CONSIDERATIONS

• Principle of loss and expense	13. Architect, progress
• Determination of employment	13. Architect, disturbance
	13. Contractor
• Hostilities and war damage	
• Antiquities	
• Other remedies	

COMMENTS ON CLAUSES

• Loss and expense	14. Reimbursement for loss and expense
• limited definition	
• when invoked	

- procedure to calculate
- nominated sub-con-
  tractors
- Differences between determination by employer and
  contractor
  - in principle
  - procedures
  - defaults causing
- Completion and settlement
  when employer determines
- Settlement only when contractor determines
- Hostilities and war damage
  - completion or determi-
    nation
  - settlement
- Antiquities
  - action
  - reimbursement

14. Determination of con-
    tractor's employment

14. Example of financial
    settlement

Chapter 8: Injury to persons and property
(*Clauses 20–22*)

GENERAL CONSIDERATIONS

- Scope of injury
- Indemnity
- Insurance to cover generally
- Insurance when not neg-
  ligence
- Non-insurable elements
- Insurance of works
  - alternative clauses
  - possible determination
- Employer's loss not men-
  tioned

13. Contractor, related re-
    sponsibilities
13. Architect, disturbance
13. Architect, insurances
14. Indemnity, injury and
    insurance

COMMENTS ON CLAUSES
- Scope of indemnity and
  insurance
- Extent of insurance

- Remedies for failure to insure
- Insurance when not negligence
- Non-insurable elements
- Insurance of works, alternatives
  - common elements
  - different elements
  - comparison of settlements
- Other relief available

Chapter 9: Variations and fluctuations
(*Clauses 13, 37–40*)

GENERAL CONSIDERATIONS

- Three classes of adjustment
  - variations
  - claims (considered elsewhere)
  - fluctuations

13. Quantity surveyor
15. Contract sum and adjustment

COMMENTS ON CLAUSES

- Scope of variations
  - inclusive and exclusive
  - how introduced
- Provisional sums
- Valuation of both last
- Fluctuations, main comparative principles of reimbursement
  - by cost
    - statutory elements
    - market elements
  - by value, formula method
- Details of statutory and market fluctuations
  - labour etc.
  - materials etc.
  - domestic sub-contractors
  - procedures and definitions
- Details of formula fluctuations

- ground rules
- timetable
- corrections
- provisos etc.

Chapter 10: Interim payments and final settlement
(*Clauses 16, 30*)

GENERAL CONSIDERATIONS

13. Contractor, related responsibilities
13. Contractor, contract rights
13. Quantity surveyor

- Modification of entirety principle
  - payment pattern
- Adjustments of contract sum mostly in clause 30
- Method of interim valuation open
- Materials included in interim amounts
  - on/off-site
  - subject to title
- Nominated sub-contractors' special treatment
- Retention
- Final certificate alone 'final'

COMMENTS ON CLAUSES
- Timetable
  - interim certificates
  - stage payments
  - reduction of retention
  - final amounts for nominated sub-contractors
  - final certificate
- Interim calculations
  - who prepares
  - gross and net items
  - to include variations etc.
  - off-site materials
  - employer deductions ignored
- Final calculations

13. Architect, interim payments
15. Timing of interim payments

15. Main elements of interim payments

15. Deductions by employer

13. Architect, final payments

- exchange of information
- deduction and addition elements
- final account leads to final certificate amount
- Safeguards for employer
- retention on work of
  - contractor
  - nominated sub-contractors
  - materials on/off-site
- Safeguards for nominated sub-contractors
  - control of
    - amounts
    - retention
  - direct interim payment
  - final early payment
- Final settlement
  - finance
    - statement
    - errors
  - quality
    - as contract
    - reasonable satisfaction
- Effect of final certificate
  - finality
  - proceedings

15. Final payment

15. Retention on interim payments

15. Payments, nominated subcontractors

15. Final payment
15. Final certificate

15. Proceedings
15. Arbitration

SUMMARIES OF CHAPTERS IN PART 3

See the beginning of this chapter for the way in which these lists may be used.

Chapter 13: Persons and organisations
- Persons and bodies
  - persons
  - bodies
- Employer
  - contract obligations
  - contract rights
- Contractor
  - performance obligations

- related responsibilities
- contract rights
- contract liabilities
- Architect
  - clause references for instructions, orders etc.
    - instructions over various matters
    - instructions over nominated persons
    - 'deemed' variations, not requiring instructions
    - other classes of directions
    - confirmation of matters
  - clause references for certificates
  - other documents from architect
  - design and quality
  - progress
  - disturbance
  - insurances
  - other persons working
  - interim payments
  - final payments
- Quantity surveyor
  - contract duties
- Sub-contractors and suppliers
  - procedures for appointment
  - procedures during progress
  - some general principles over sub-contractors and suppliers
  - main differences between treatment of nominated sub-contractors and nominated suppliers in contract
  - references to sub-contractors and suppliers in contract, other than in clauses 19, 35 and 36
  - some differences between JCT main contract and JCT nominated sub-contract
  - significant provisions in the employer/nominated sub-contractor agreements

Chapter 14: Works and progress
- Documents
  - contract documents
  - post-contract documents
- Works and site
  - scope of works
  - execution of works
  - site of works
- Progress and disturbance
  - standard pattern of progress
  - disturbance of standard pattern

- extension of completion time
- reimbursement for loss and expense
- determination of contractor's employment
- causes of delay leading to extension, reimbursement or determination in favour of contractor
- example of financial settlement when employer determines under clause 27
- Indemnity, injury and insurance
  - indemnity
  - injury
  - insurance
  - procedures for reinstatement and settlement under clause 22

Chapter 15: Finance and finalisation

- Contract sum and adjustment
  - contract sum
  - adjustments of contract sum
  - financial adjustments other than by adjustment of contract sum
  - rules for calculating adjustments
- Payments
  - timing of interim payments
  - main elements of interim payments
  - retention on interim payments
  - nominated sub-contractors
  - final payment
  - deductions by employer
  - Example of deductions for direct payments to nominated sub-contractors
  - Example of retention allocations at partial possession during a contract
- Completion and settlement
  - physical completion
  - financial settlement
  - final certificate
  - proceedings
  - arbitration

CHAPTER 13

PERSONS AND ORGANISATIONS

PERSONS AND BODIES

The lists give all those named in the articles and conditions, placing them in their major relationships and giving clause references only when they are of single or infrequent occurrence. The most common of the persons are treated separately in the remaining parts of this chapter.

Persons	Clause refs
● Employer	—
● architect	—
● architect's representatives	11
● quantity surveyor	—
● clerk of works	12, 34.1.3
● persons employed or otherwise engaged by employer	25.4.8, 26.2.4, 29
● third party dealing with antiquities	34.2
● persons for whom employer is responsible (who include the foregoing)	20.1, 21.1
● Contractor	—
● person-in-charge	10
● servants or agents	
● sub-contractors in general, and their servants or agents	—
● domestic sub-contractors	19.2–19.4, 38.3, 39.4, 40.4.2
● nominated sub-contractors	—
● sub-contractors and suppliers in general	27.4.2, 28.2.1
● nominated suppliers	—
● workpeople	particularly in 38 and 39
● Insurers, related to various of foregoing	—

Bodies	
● Local authorities and statutory undertakers	6, 25.4.11

- The Crown   32.1
- United Kingdom Government   25.4.9
- Commissioners of Customs and Excise   15
- Royal Institute of British Architects   Art. 5.1
  (RIBA)
- Royal Institution of Chartered Surveyors   13.5.4
- National Federation of Building Trades   13.5.4
  Employers
- National Joint Council for the Building   38.1, 39.1
  Industry and other wage-fixing bodies

EMPLOYER

The employer is largely passive under the contract, although he is one of the only two parties to the contract. Most actions are performed by the architect on his behalf, or in deciding between the employer and the contractor.

Contract obligations	*Clause refs*
• Implied	—
• providing legality of works, e.g. planning permission	—
• making site available for works	—
• keeping clear of site, subject to any work he performs	—
• finding funds for works progressively	—
• receiving certificates etc. from architect	—
• meeting injury claims etc. not the liability of contractor	—
• Expressed	—
• agreeing any supplement to list of possible domestic sub-contractors	19.3
• insuring works etc. as contract option	22B, 22C
• meeting amounts of interim and final certificates	30.1.1.1, 30.8
• paying nominated sub-contractors direct	35.13.5
• if contractor defaults, only	—
• perhaps on discretionary basis	—

Contract rights
- Receipt of completed works from   17
  contractor

CONTRACTOR

The contractor is the other party to the contract and obviously is very active. While the following sections give his distinctive aspects, undue repetition has been avoided by giving detailed points under headings later in this chapter and in those following.

Performance obligations   *Clause refs*

- Carrying out and completing works — 2.1
  - whole construction activity — —
  - but not design (see 'Architect' and —
'Nominated sub-contractors')
- Conforming to/complying with — —
  - contract drawings over design of · 2.1
works, amplified by
    - descriptive schedules — 5.3
    - further drawings or details — 5.4
    - levels and setting out information — 7
  - contract bills over quality of works — 2.1, 14.1
  - statutory requirements — 6.1
- Obeying instructions — 4.1.1
  - see list under 'Architect' — —
  - received in writing, perhaps by — 4.3, 10, 12
person-in-charge, or confirmed by
contractor, not from clerk of works
  - requested by contractor, if not given — 25.4.6, 26.2.1
when needed
  - but may be queried whether — 4.2
empowered
  - if not obeyed, employer may — —
    - bring in others to perform over — 4.1.2
defaults
    - determine contractor's employment — 27.1.3
over serious instances
- Workmanlike activity over — —
  - organisation of works — 2.1, 23.1
    - including domestic and nominated — —
sub-contracts
    - producing and revising master — 5.3.1.2
programme if required
  - seeking information, instructions etc. — 2.3, 25.4.6,
reasonably seen to be required — 26.2.1
  - regular and diligent progress — 23.1
- Delivering up completed works — —
  - in their entirety, despite damage and — 2.1
other hazards
  - correct in disposition and quality — 2.1
  - on time, subject to permitted — 23.1
extensions
  - remedying defects found in defects — 17.2, 17.3
liability period

- meeting residual liabilities over defects before and after final certificate   30.9

Related responsibilities
- Indemnifying employer within limits given over   —
  - royalties and patent rights included in contract sum   9.1
  - injury to persons   20.1
  - injury to property in general, *including* works and materials   20.2
- Insuring against injury   —
  - in support of indemnities   —
    - persons, including employees, to statutory level   21.1
    - property in general, to level in appendix   21.1
    - works and materials on site against clause 22 perils   22A
    - any off-site materials paid for by employer against all risks   16.2
    - but *not* works and materials on site against clause 22 perils when employer responsible   22B, 22C
  - in absence of indemnity and liability   —
    - property against special classes of damage   21.2
- Funding operations   —
  - by paying   —
    - his own organisation   —
    - all sub-contractors and suppliers   —
      - but only paying nominated sub-contractors as and when directed   35.13.1, 35.13.2
  - while being paid at all times given   30.1
- Co-operating over final account   —
  - preparing daywork records   13.5.4
  - attending for measurements, if he so wishes   13.6
  - providing documents for adjusting contract sum   30.6.1

Contract rights
- Access to and exclusive possession of site, subject to   23.1

- phased possession, not considered in conditions but possible — —
- phased completion, by either/both — —
  - sectional completion as supplementary contract condition — SCS
  - partial (re)possession, arising by later agreement — 18
- restrictions in contract bills over — —
  - access to site — 13.1.2
  - use of parts of site — 13.1.2
  - working space — 13.1.2
  - working hours — 13.1.2
  - order of work — 13.1.2
  - ingress and egress through other land etc. — 25.4.12, 26.2.6
- employer doing working or engaging others to work on site — —
  - as detailed in contract bills, or — 29.1
  - as agreed during progress — 29.2
- Information regarding works to allow proper progress — —
  - documents generally (see 'Documents') — 5
  - particularly instructions that architect *must* issue — 4.1, 25.4.6, 26.2.1
- Planning and control of own activities — 2.1
  - programme of work, subject to — 23.1
    - restrictions, listed above — 13.1.2 etc.
    - providing and revising master programme — 5.3.1.2
      - if required — —-
      - but without obligation to change or observe it — —
    - requesting information in time — 25.4.6, 26.2.1
  - performing work himself, or sub-contracting it, subject to — —
    - permission to sub-let generally — 19.2
    - obligation to sub-let, if contract bills require — 19.3
    - obligation to accept nomination of sub-contractors or suppliers — 35.1, 36.1
      - if contract bills give prime cost sum for particular types of work — —
      - if similar work arises post-contractually in defined ways — —

- methods of producing finished work, subject to specification in contract bills — 2.1, 14.1
- Programme revisions — —
  - extension of time due to 'relevant events' — 25.4
  - early termination (determination) for — —
    - breaches by employer — 28.1.1, 28.1.2
    - specified major delays — 28.1.3
    - insolvency of employer — 28.1.4
- Adjustment of contract sum (see Ch. 15), broadly — —
  - variations of works — 13
  - loss and expense and other claims — 26 etc.
  - damage covered by employer's insurance — 22B, 22C
  - fluctuations in costs — 38, 39, 40
- Payment of adjusted contract sum (see Ch. 15), broadly — —
  - on account during and after progress, subject to retention — 30.1–30.4
  - reduction of retention at — 30.4
    - sectional completion — SCS
    - partial possession — 18
    - practical completion — 17
    - making good defects, after each of foregoing — SCS, 18, 17
  - special final amounts for nominated sub-contractors — 30.7, 35.17
  - final balance at final certificate — 30.8
- Certified satisfaction of architect with works — 30.9.1
- Arbitration or other proceedings — —
  - over disputes — Art. 5
  - provided started in due time — 30.9.2, 30.9.3

Contract liabilities

These are largely the reverse of the 'Contract rights' given under 'Employer'.

ARCHITECT

See for this section in particular Chapter 1 regarding 'Special provisions of building contracts'.

Instructions, orders etc.

These must be written instructions etc. unless 'deemed'. They may be classified as:

- To permit execution, e.g. over nomination
- To secure compliance, e.g. over defects
- To clarify matters, e.g. over discrepancies
- Optional, e.g. over variations

INSTRUCTIONS OVER VARIOUS MATTERS	*Clause refs*
• Discrepancies or divergences	2.3
• Statutory obligations	6.1.3
• Setting out works	7
• Opening up and testing	8.3
• Removal of defective work etc.	8.4
• Exclusion of persons	8.5
• Variations	13.2
• Expenditure of provisional sums	13.3
• Defects during defects liability period	17.3
• Removal of debris after damage	22C.2.3.2
• Postponement of work	23.2
• Documents to quantity surveyor	30.6.1.1
• Protective work during hostilities	32.2
• War damage	33.1.2
• Antiquities	34.2

INSTRUCTIONS OVER NOMINATED PERSONS	
• Change of procedure	35.5.2
• Failure to agree details	35.8
• Nomination by 'basic' method	35.10.2
• Nomination by 'alternative' method	35.11.2
• Nomination of substituted sub-contractor	35.18.1.1
• Default of sub-contractor	35.24.4.1
• Nomination of supplier	36.2

'DEEMED' VARIATIONS, NOT REQUIRING INSTRUCTIONS	
• Correction of contract bills	2.2.2.2.
• Statutory obligations	6.1.4.3
• Restoration and removal of debris after damage	22B.2.2
• Ditto	22C.2.3.3

- Incomplete work at determination　　28.2.2.2
- Work after war damage　　33.1.4

OTHER CLASSES OF DIRECTIVES
- Clerk of works' directions　　12
- Schedule of defects　　17.2
- Quantity surveyor to ascertain loss and　　26.1
  expense due to disturbance
- Notice of determination　　27.1
- Removal of plant etc.　　27.4.3
- Quantity surveyor to ascertain loss and　　34.3.1
  expense due to antiquities
- Payment of nominated sub-contractors　　35.13.1.1
- Ditto at determination　　35.26

CONFIRMATION OF MATTERS
- Architect's oral instructions　　4.3.2
- Building inspector's and others' oral or　　6.1
  written requirements
- Clerk of works' oral or written directions　　12
- Variations other than by architect's　　13.2
  instructions

CERTIFICATES
(see Ch. 1 under 'Certificates')
- Practical completion of works　　17.1
- Completion of making good defects after　　17.4
  practical completion
- Estimate of approximate value at partial　　18.1.1
  possession
- Completion of making good defects after　　18.1.3
  partial possession
- Payment of insurance monies after　　22A.4.2
  damage reinstatement
- Failure to complete works　　24.1
- Expenses and loss and/or damage arising　　27.4.4
  out of determination
- Interim certificates generally　　30.1.1.1
- Interim certificates to pay off nominated　　30.7, 35.17
  sub-contractors
- Final certificate　　30.8
- Failure to prove payment of　　35.13.5.2
  sub-contractors
- Failure of sub-contractors to complete　　35.15.1

- Practical completion of sub-contract   35.16
  work

Other documents from architect
(see 'Contract documents' and 'Post-contract documents' under
'Documents' in Ch. 14)

Design and quality
(see Ch. 3 under 'Architect's actions')
The architect is entirely responsible for establishing both of these;
the contractor is then responsible for producing the works in conformity with them. Key elements are:

	Clause refs
• Articles of agreement refer to architect	Art. 3
• pre-contractually and post-contractually	—
• need not be same person	—
• Specialist design may be	—
• by consultants, who are unmentioned but subsumed under architect in contract, or	—
• by nominated persons, who are not responsible to contractor for design	—
• Documents (see separate heading of 'Documents' for detail) convey	—
• design, mainly by contract drawings	2.1
• quality, mainly by contract bills	2.1, 14.1
• statutory matters, by either means	6.1
• post-contract matters, including variations, by instructions	4.1
• Setting out and levels	7
• information by architect, but	—
• work by contractor	—
• Architect has right of inspection, including	—
• access to work and workshops	11
• working through clerk of works	12
• opening up and testing	8.3
• instructing removal of defective work and materials	8.4
• Defects	—
• may be condemned	—
• during progress	8.4

● during defects liability period	17.2, 17.3
● thereafter contractor	—
● liable for cost of remedying	—
● not necessarily for doing work himself	—
● Final certificate alone expresses satisfaction that works conform to contract	30.9.1, 30.10
● Arbitration usually possible only between practical completion and final certificate	Art. 5

Progress
(see 'Progress' in Ch. 14)
It is primarily the contractor's responsibility to meet the completion date and he should warn the architect about lack of information and instructions. The architect has responsibilities over:

	Clause refs
● Information being in time	—
● e.g. levels and drawings	—
● Instructions or lack of them may hinder progress	—
● e.g. postponement, variations (including over site restrictions and obligations), resolving discrepancies	—
● Extension of time related to	—
● specific causes	25.4
● defined procedures	25.2
● his agreement	25.3
● Regularity of progress must be monitored in relation to	23.1
● extension of time	25.3.4
● determination	27.1
● Acceleration of programme	25.3.6
● cannot be instructed	—
● even when time has been lost	—
● Certifying non-completion	24.1
● leading to application of liquidated damages provision	24.2
● Certifying practical completion, or	17.1
● a measure of it at partial possession or sectional completion	—

Disturbance
(see 'Progress' in Ch. 14)
The last section relates to ordinary progress and delay. The
architect has particular responsibilities in other cases:

	Clause refs
• Damage to works, architect	22A, 22B, 22C
• certifies payments to contractor	—
• otherwise conditions say little	—
• although by implication architect supervises reinstatement as though is 'first time' work	—
• Determination by employer, architect	27
• issues notices	—
• deals (although not mentioned) with completion of works	—
• orders off contractor's property	—
• settles up accounts (in practice with quantity surveyor)	—
• Determination by contractor, architect	28
• receives notice	—
• oversees (although not mentioned) contractor's removal	—
• settles up accounts (again with quantity surveyor)	—
• especially those of nominated sub-contractors	—
• Discovery of antiquities, architect	33
• issues instructions	—
• deals with loss and expense	—
• Renomination of nominated sub-contractor for any of several reasons, architect	35.24
• must deal completely	—
• as usual, with variations in procedures	—

Insurances
Responsibility to insure lies with the employer or contractor, but
the architect has certain specified duties, as well as the duty of
supervising completion of the works after damage:

	Clause refs
• Checking that insurances maintained	—

by contractor and on policies and
premiums over

• persons and property generally	21.1
• works, if by running policy	22A
• Approving insurers and receiving policies over	—
• property, special risks	21.2
• works, if by individual policy	22A
• Certifying insurance settlement payments as such	22A
• Receiving notice of damage and certifying variation payments	22B, 22C
• Instructing removal of debris	22C

Other persons working

In the first three cases, the contractor controls their activities and
the architect may instruct them only through the contractor and
only when they are appointed. In the last case, the contractor has
no control and the architect *may* not have any (conditions are
silent). The architect has responsibilities over certain issues:

	Clause refs
• Domestic sub-contractors for sub-let work	—
• partial control of selection by	—
• naming in contract bills, or	19.3
• approval post-contractually	19.2
• rights over	—
• access to workshops	11
• notice about fluctuations	38.3, 39.4
• Nominated sub-contractors	—
• selecting, nominating and dealing with them	—
• as extensive list of elements in 'General considerations' in Chapter 5	—
• actions during progress under Agreement NSC/2 and Sub-Contract NSC/4	—
• especially over payment and their safeguarding	—
• co-ordinating design work outside scope of conditions	—
• Nominated suppliers	—
• selecting and, if required, concluding warranty	36.1

- nominating   36.2
- approving any related extra costs of   36.3
  contractor
- Others engaged by employer   —
  - giving information in contract bills   29.1
  - dealing with any disturbance effects   25.4.8, 26.2.4
    on contractor

Interim payments
(see Ch. 15)
The architect is responsible for certifying these, with the following main considerations:

	Clause refs
• Frequency stipulated in appendix	30.1.3
• Interim valuation by quantity surveyor	—
• usually at architect's discretion, but	30.1.2
• obligatory if formula fluctuations apply	40.2
• Amounts to be included	—
• elements specified	30.2
• which of them subject to retention	—
• materials off-site optional	30.3
• subject to special provisions	—
• Retention	—
• to be divided between contractor and nominated sub-contractors	30.4
• if requested put in a trust fund by employer	30.5
• to be reduced on specific happenings	30.4
• Estimate by architect required at partial possession or sectional completion to enable reduction of retention, *inter alia*	18.1.1, SCS
• Nominated sub-contractors are dealt with specially, by	—
• direction to contractor as to amounts	35.13.1
• notifying these to sub-contractors	—
• checking that these have been paid	35.13.3
• if not, powers of direct payment, possibly optional	35.13.5

- Employer may deduct from payments,   30.1.1.2
  including payments of retention, any
  amounts allowed by conditions (see
  list and example in Ch. 15)
  - architect   —
    - may advise him of these   —
    - but must not deduct them in   —
      calculating amounts certified

Final payments
The architect is not responsible for calculating adjustments to the
contract sum on which final payment is made, unless he reserves
this to himself as he may in some cases (see clauses 26.1 and
34.3). Otherwise his main responsibilities are:

	Clause refs
• Confirmation of any outstanding instructions	4.3.2
• Receiving documents for final account from contractor	30.6.1
• to make comments before passing to quantity surveyor	—
• Certifying final payments to nominated sub-contractors	—
• ahead of final certificate	30.7, 35.17
• checking have been made	35.13.3
• otherwise advising employer over direct payments	35.13.5
• as with interim amounts	—
• Issuing final certificate	30.8
• which, *inter alia*, notifies final payment	—
• Advising employer about	30.8
• any deductions from final payment which he may make	—
• but not deducting them when calculating final payment shown in final certificate	—
• Preparing for any proceedings intimated before or within 14 days of final certificate	30.9.2, 30.9.3

QUANTITY SURVEYOR

The quantity surveyor is named in the articles of agreement and in the conditions he is mentioned mainly over:

- Interim payments: centring in interim valuations, which are passed to the architect to form the basis of his interim certificates
- Final adjustment of the contract sum: centring in what is usually termed the final account (an expression not used in the conditions), which forms the basis of the figures in the architect's final certificate

Contract duties	*Clause refs*
• Optional custodian of contract documents	5.1
• Valuation of variations and provisional sum expenditure	13.4
• Allowing contractor to be present at measurement	13.6
• Ascertaining amounts of loss and expense, if architect instructs	26.1
• Preparing interim valuations	30.1
• usually, if architect considers them necessary	—
• always, if clause 40 fluctuations apply	—
• Preparing statements of retention, if architect instructs	30.5
• Preparing statement of final valuation of variations	30.6
• Preparing adjustment of contract sum, including last statement, by implication	30.6
• Calculation of all fluctuations, by implication	38, 39, 40
• Final agreement of any part of fluctuations	38, 39
• Agreement of alteration to methods of calculating fluctuations	40

SUB-CONTRACTORS AND SUPPLIERS

The conditions include references to the following types:

- Domestic sub-contractors
- Nominated sub-contractors

- Nominated suppliers

There are *not* references to domestic suppliers, although suppliers in general are mentioned. The sections below deal only with the three specific types. All three are the full contractual responsibility of the contractor, as against those other persons under direct contract with the employer.

Procedures for appointment	*Clause refs*
• Domestic sub-contractors	19.1
• two methods	—
• contractor's choice post-contractually, subject to architect's consent	19.2
• not unreasonably withheld	—
• except over sub-letting work in lieu of nominated sub-contract	—
• list of persons in contract bills	19.3
• contractor chooses from this, not subject to consent	—
• if list shrinks, there is procedure to supplement	—
• in neither method does	—
• architect issue documents or obtain tenders	—
• price payable to contractor change from what is in contract bills	—
• Nominated sub-contractors	—
• overall process given in Chapter 5	—
• clause 35 covers	—
• definition, i.e. pre-conditions permitting nomination to occur	35.1
• alternative of contractor performing nominated work	35.2
• right of contractor to object to proposed person, and time limit	35.4
• basic method of nomination: main actions after architect made his selection	35.6–35.10
• architect sends documents to contractor	—
• contractor treats with proposed sub-contractor over details	—

amounts, by including in
interim certificates
- architect informs nominated   —
  sub-contractors of amounts
- contractor pays nominated   —
  sub-contractors
- architect checks payments   —
  before next interim certificate
- if not made, without adequate   —
  reason
  - employer may pay direct   —
    and deduct from next
    interim certificate
    - obligatory if   —
      employer/nominated
      sub-contractor
      agreement in use
    - otherwise optional   —
  - subject to   —
    - several rules and   —
    - to employer not being   —
      out of pocket
  - does *not* extend to paying   —
    direct *before* default
- contractor granting extension of   35.14
  time to nominated
  sub-contractors
  - only with architect's consent   —
  - architect to observe terms of   —
    sub-contract
  - this links with extension of   —
    time for contractor over
    nominated sub-contractor's
    delay
- architect certifying to contractor   —
  - failure of nominated   35.15
    sub-contractor to complete on
    time, in whole or parts
  - practical completion of   35.16
    nominated sub-contract
    works, in whole
- final payments   35.17–35.19
  - architect to include in interim   —
    certificates
    - at latest 12 months after   —

Some general principles over sub-contractors and suppliers
- Contractor entirely responsible for   —

them, even if nominated, unless
conditions say otherwise
- organising and programming work   —
- performance and quality of work   —
- meeting damages etc. and   —
  recovering from them if
  appropriate
- Contractor *not* responsible for design   —
  by them
  - such design *not* mentioned in   —
    contract or in sub-contracts
  - but covered in employer/nominated   —
    sub-contractor agreement and
    nominated supplier warranty
- Architect *not* to instruct or   —
  communicate with them direct
  - after any nomination   —
  - at all if domestic   —
  - except over design matters   —
  - even on nominated sub-contractors'   —
    payments and programme, acts
    through contractor
- Quantity surveyor *not* to treat with   —
  them direct
  - except (by implication) over   —
    nominated sub-contractors' final
    accounts with contractor's consent
- Work by domestic sub-contractors   —
  paid for
  - by employer at contractor's prices   —
    in contract bills, without change or
    addition
  - by contractor at prices in the   —
    domestic sub-contract
- Insurance of liabilities   —
  - contractor, sub-contractors and   —
    suppliers all responsible for own
    insurances
  - *except that* contractor or employer   —
    insures against clause 22 perils only
    to cover
    - work executed and materials on   —
      site
    - but *not* temporary items and   —
      plant

Main differences between treatment of nominated sub-contractors and nominated suppliers in contract

These are listed under 'General considerations over suppliers' in Chapter 5.

References to sub-contractors and suppliers in contract, other than in clauses 19, 35 and 36

These highlight differences in treatment of the various types and the terms used below are therefore precise and significant in indicating which types are in question.

	Clause refs
• Joint arbitration with contractor for nominated persons	Art. 5
• Local authority or statutory undertaker, not a sub-contractor	6.3
• Access to workshops of domestic and nominated sub-contractors	11
• Contractor's work not to become nominated sub-contractor's work	13.1.3
• Provisional sums in sub-contracts	13.3.2
• Variations in nominated sub-contracts	13.4.1
• Distinction between domestic and nominated sub-contractors	19.2, 19.5
• Injury and insurance regarding sub-contracts	20, 21
• Extension of time advised to nominated sub-contractors	25.2, 25.3.5
• Delay on part of nominated sub-contractors and nominated suppliers	25.4.7
• Loss and expense of nominated sub-contractors	26.4
• Assignment and payment of sub-contractors and suppliers at main contract determination	27.4.2
• Settling nominated sub-contracts at same	28.2.3
• Interim amounts for nominated sub-contractors	30.2
• Off-site materials of sub-contractors	30.3
• Division of retention between contractor and nominated sub-contractors	30.4.2
• Rules over treatment of last	30.5
• Nominated sub-contract final account documents	30.6.1
• Nominated sub-contracts and nominated	30.6.2

supplies in adjustment of contract sum

● Final payment of nominated sub-contractors	30.7
● Domestic sub-contractors' fluctuations	38.3, 39.4
● Nominated sub-contractors' and nominated suppliers' fluctuations not covered	38.5.2, 39.6.2
● Contractor's fluctuations not covered when in work in lieu of nomination	38.5.3, 39.6.3
● Nominated sub-contractors' fluctuations	40.4.1
● Domestic sub-contractors' fluctuations	40.4.2
● Contractor wishing to tender for nominated sub-contract work	Appendix

Some differences between JCT main contract and JCT nominated sub-contracts

The particular topic given below for a clause indicates the difference from the main contract. It may not be the title or even the main subject of the clause.

	Clause refs
● Sub-contractor's liabilities incorporated from main contract	5
● Cross-indemnities between contractor and sub-contractor	6
● Sub-contractor not to insure against clause 22 perils	8
● Sub-contractor responsible for own plant etc.	10
● Loss and expense, extra provisions between contractor and sub-contractor only	13
● Sub-contract price, with either variations or complete remeasurement	15, 16, 17
● VAT to be included *in* sub-contract amount	19A, 19B
● Contractor's right to set off against payments to sub-contractor	23
● Appointment of adjudicator over last	24
● Attendance by contractor on sub-contractor	27
● Contractor and sub-contractor not to misuse each other's property	28
● Determination under sub-contract by contractor	29

- Determination under sub-contract by   30
  sub-contractor
- Determination under main contract by   31
  either party
- Loss and expense due to strikes etc.   33

Significant provisions in the employer/nominated sub-contractor agreements
The two documents are Agreement NSC/2 relating to the basic method of nomination and Agreement NSC/2a relating to the alternative method. Clause references are to the former.

Clause refs

- Architect not liable to sub-contractor by   Recital
  virtue of the agreement
- Design and specification responsibility of   2.1
  sub-contractor, over quality and
  programme
- Direct payment for work before   2.2
  nomination
- Sub-contractor liable to employer over   3
  extension of time, loss and expense and
  determination of sub-contract when
  contractor not liable
- Direct payment of sub-contractor by   4, 7
  employer after contractor's failure in
  paying
- Early final payment of sub-contractor,   5
  subject to continuing liability for defects

CHAPTER 14

WORKS AND PROGRESS

DOCUMENTS

All the important documents are listed here, or reference is made to lists elsewhere. By definition, all these items must contain written or graphic information and the subject-matter of the communication will be invalid if the attempt is made to leave it oral.

The effect of some of these documents is given under other headings. Documents relating to VAT and other financial legislation have not been given.

Contract documents	Clause refs
• The JCT form consists of three contract documents	2.1
• articles of agreement	—
• conditions	—
• appendix	—
• The three above are to prevail over the other two types below if there is any divergence	2.2.1
• While no discrepancy within them is assumed by their wording, they contain alternatives and have spaces for insertions which must be dealt with to make the contract workable	—
• The other two types of contract documents are	—
• contract drawings listed in the articles of agreement	5.2.1, 5.2.2
• contract bills, described in the articles of agreement as fully priced	5.2.1
• Contents of the contract drawings are usually not elaborated upon in the conditions	—
• Those of the contract bills are to include when appropriate	—
• quality and quantity of works	14.1
• departures from SMM	2.2.2
• obligations or restrictions imposed by	13.1.2

employer
- ingress to or egress from site (may   25.4.12, 26.2.6
  also be on contract drawings)
- daywork terms   13.5.4
- lists of domestic sub-contractors   19.3
- prime cost sums and/or names for   35.1
  nominated sub-contractors
- nomination methods for   35.5.1
  sub-contractors and whether
  Agreement NSC/2a required
- information about work by employer   29.1
  or those he engages etc.
- prime cost sums for nominated   36.1
  suppliers
- provisional sums   13.3
- special provisional sum for joint   21.2
  insurance of property
- datum from which fluctuations   38.1, 38.2, 39.1,
  adjustments start   39.3
- list of imported materials under   40.3
  formula fluctuations
- The contract bills cannot themselves   2.2.1
  amend the conditions, only give warning
  of intended amendments

Post-contract documents
- Drawings and details   —
  - amplifying, but not amending the   5.4
    contract drawings
  - giving levels and setting out   7
    information
  - as part of variation instructions   13.2
- Descriptive schedules or other like   —
  documents
  - explaining position etc. of work   5.3.1
  - presumably as part of variation   —
    instructions, although conditions do
    not mention
  - Unpriced bills of quantities   5.2.3
- Contractor's master programme,   5.3.1
  optional
- Instructions, orders etc. (see under   4.1
  'Architect')
- Certificates (see under 'Architect')   5.8

WORKS AND SITE

Often the term 'the works' is used rather than 'the site', even when the meaning is otherwise, e.g. the person-in-charge and materials are 'on the works'.

Scope of works	*Clause refs*
● Contractor to produce entire	—
● responsible for all sub-contractors' work as part	2.1
● paid by employer	30.1
● Broad description in articles of agreement	Recitals
● Precise delineation of layout and quality in	—
● contract drawings	2.1
● contract bills	2.1, 14.1
● Amplified by	—
● drawings and details	5.4
● descriptive schedules or specification	5.3.1
● instructions over prime cost and provisional sums	35.1 etc. 36.1 etc. 13.3
● Clarified over	—
● errors etc. in contract bills	2.2
● discrepancies in and divergences between contract documents	2.3
● statutory obligations	6.1
● Altered by variations	13.1, 13.2

Execution of works	
● Contractor decides methods, subject to	—
● any site restrictions or obligations (see 'Site of works')	13.1.2
● any technical specification in contract bills, or by variation	14.1, 13.1.1
● Contractor responsible for	—
● defects during and after progress, subject to	2.1, 8.3, 17.2, 17.3
● architect's discretion over	—
● setting out and levels	7
● defects liability period	17.2, 17.3
● early release of nominated sub-contractors from liability	35.18, 35.19
● final certificate reducing liability	30.9.1
● expiry of limitations period	—
● damage to and restoration of work	2.1, 20.2

and unfixed materials, subject to any
- caused by those for whom employer responsible — 20.2
- when employer responsible for insurance *and* risk — 22B, 22C
- special cases, caused by
  - nuclear and other excepted perils — 21.3
  - war — 33.1
- delay, unless extension of time granted — 24.2

Site of works
- Defined by — —
  - insertion in articles of agreement — —
  - contract drawings — —
  - contract bills — —
  - inspection during tendering — —
- Contractor has exclusive possession during contract period, subject to — 23.1
  - any restrictions and obligations imposed in contract bills — 13.1.2
    - and any variations on these — —
    - but not introduction of a category post-contractually — —
  - rights of access reserved to — —
    - architect and his representatives, including presumably — 11
      - clerk of works — —
      - quantity surveyor — —
    - employer and others performing work not included in contract — 29
- Particular provisions relate to — —
  - levels and setting out on site — 7
  - control over and ownership of materials on site — 16.1
  - responsibility for adjoining property over special risks — 21.2
  - antiquities discovered on site — 34
- Return to employer at practical completion, with works on it — —
  - usually all at once — 17.1
  - but there may be — —
    - sectional completion, anticipated in contract — SCS

- partial possession, occurring   18.1
  post-contractually by agreement

PROGRESS AND DISTURBANCE

The implicit contract basis is that both parties and those acting
for them in any way will perform their parts on time, so as not to
prevent the works from starting, proceeding and finishing on
time. Settlement also follows in a defined way. External agencies
may disturb this programme, but the parties' liabilities can be
relaxed only as the contract provides.

Standard pattern of progress	Clause refs
• Design and all related matters, e.g. statutory approvals, assumed to be complete before work commences on site	Art. 1, 2.1
• Possession of site to be given to contractor on date for possession	23.1
• phased possession needs slight modification of conditions	—
• Contractor to proceed regularly and diligently	23.1
• in own order, unless contract bills limit him	13.1.2
• if optional master programme provided to architect, for information	5.3.1.2
• contractor not obliged to work to it	—
• although must revise it	—
• has obligation to warn architect of information which he requires in adequate time	25.4.6, 26.2.1
• Completion by contractor to be on or before completion date	23.1
• may complete whole works early, apparently by as large a margin as he chooses	—
• phased completion may occur by	—
• sectional completion required in contract	SCS
• partial early possession occurring by agreement during progress	18.1
• practical completion occurs when	17.1

whole works complete (see Ch. 6 for effects)

- After practical completion no fresh work may be instructed and there follow   —
  - defects liability period, if defects are found during this contractor obliged to remedy them   17.2, 17.3
  - interim period, during this contractor remains liable for defects, but need not remedy them himself   —
  - final certificate ending contract   30.8
  - limitations period, during which contractor liable over any remaining obligations   —

Disturbance of standard pattern

- Contractor must finish on time and without extra reimbursement   23.1
  - subject to
    - extension of completion time   25
    - reimbursement of loss and expense   26
    - determination of contractor's employment   27, 28
    - any other rights and remedies he has, e.g. arbitration and court action   Art. 5
  - otherwise liable for liquidated damages   24.2
    - and possibly under other rights and remedies of employer   Art. 5

Extension of completion time

- This may be granted to contractor by architect   —
  - for whole works, or for sections, but only if these defined in contract   SCS
  - on account of specified events only, and possibly abated by effect of omissions (see 'Causes' hereafter)   25.4
- Contractor must apply under defined procedure to initiate matters and supply data   25.2
- Architect then to follow defined procedure and fix any extension   —
  - on interim basis, during progress   25.3.1, 25.3.2

- finally, within limited time of completion   25.3.3
- Provisos   —
  - contractor to work to limit delay reasonably   25.3.4
  - no date earlier than original completion date may be required of the contractor   25.3.6
  - extension of time and loss and expense do not necessarily go together   —

Reimbursement for loss and expense
- This may be granted to contractor by architect only if due to   —
  - list of specified matters (see 'Causes' hereafter)   26.2
  - antiquities   34.3
- Contractor must apply under defined procedure to initiate matters, except over antiquities, and supply data   26.1
- Architect to   26.1
  - adjudicate on claim in principle   —
  - ascertain amount, or instruct quantity surveyor to do so   —
- Important criteria   —
  - limitation to *direct* loss and expense   26.1
  - result must be material disturbance of regular progress, evidenced by any appropriate means (e.g. master programme)   26.1
  - reimbursement only of amounts not covered elsewhere in conditions, e.g. *not* to cover variations   26.1
  - possible relevance of extension of time, although again there need not be a link   26.3

Determination of contractor's employment
- This may be initiated   —
  - by either party if   —
    - damage to work etc. when works extension or alteration   22C.2.2
    - hostilities with/without war damage   32.1
  - by employer, if contractor   —
    - defaults in specified ways   27.1

- becomes insolvent, although   27.2
  - clause may be invalid   —
  - reinstatement may be agreed   —
- by contractor, if   —
  - employer   —
    - defaults in specified ways   28.1
    - becomes insolvent   28.3
  - substantial suspension of progress   28.2
    occurs for specified reasons (see
    'Causes' hereafter)
- Procedure if employer determines for   27.4
  contractor's default or insolvency
  - employer to secure completion of   —
    works
    - using contractor's materials, plant   —
      etc. on site without charge
    - securing assignment of   —
      sub-contracts etc. to self or new
      contractor
    - paying completion costs   —
  - contractor to remove surplus   —
    materials, plant etc.
  - no payment due to contractor until   —
    completion
  - balance of indebtedness to be   —
    calculated and settled (see 'Example'
    hereafter)
  - possibility of employer not wishing to   —
    complete not considered
- Procedure in all other cases   28.2
  - contractor to remove materials not   —
    paid for, plant etc.
  - employer to pay contractor for work,   —
    materials and removal in all cases
  - employer to pay contractor also for   —
    loss/damage when contractor has
    determined due to employer's default
    or insolvency, or to suspension
  - payment due as soon as ascertained   —
  - completion of works not considered   —

Causes of delay leading to extension, reimbursement or determination in favour of contractor
The following table is restricted to *delay* under the three clauses and does not include other matters leading to relief or redress for

the contractor. The precise wording and effect of the clauses differs slightly in a few instances.

Cause	Extension clause 25	Reimbursement clause 26	Determination clause 28
• Exceptional weather	yes	no	no
• Strikes, lock-outs etc.	yes	no	no
• Delay by nominated firms	yes	no	no
• Delay by statutory bodies	yes	no	no
• Liability to obtain labour, goods or materials	yes	no	no
• Exercise of statutory powers	yes	no	no
• Action on discovery of antiquities	yes	no	no
• *Force majeure*	yes	no	yes
• Fire, flood, storm etc.	yes	no	yes
• Civil commotion	yes	no	yes
• Lack of ingress/egress	yes	yes	no
• Architect's variation orders	yes	yes	yes
• Discrepancies leading to architect's instructions	yes	yes	yes
• Postponement on architect's instructions	yes	yes	yes
• Delay in obtaining drawings, instructions etc.	yes	yes	yes
• Delay by others engaged by employer	yes	yes	yes
• Opening up and testing	yes	yes	yes

Example of financial settlement when employer determines under clause 27

It is necessary to produce an account for the works as though the original contractor has finished them without interruption at his contract terms. This may be taken as follows:

Contract sum	220,000
Net addition for variations, fluctuations etc.	20,000
Hypothetical final account	£240,00

At and following upon determination, the following amounts are paid:

Interim certificates	140,000
Less retention 5%	7,000
	133,000
Part of above retention held in trust for and eventually paid to nominated sub-contractors	2,000
Expended under original contract	£135,000

It is not necessary to prepare a precise account for the value of work at determination to enable the final liabilities to be settled. To the extent, if any, that such an account revealed that the value exceeded the above it would indicate what was actually in hand to help reduce the balance shown below. It would consist essentially of the retention and any inaccuracy in the interim certificates.

All amounts paid by the employer are to be summated and set against the amount that he should have spent. These elements are as follows:

Expended under original contract	135,000
Expended to complete works	113,000
Employer's loss and expense	7,000
	£255,000
Less hypothetical final account	240,000
Net indebtedness of contractor	£15,000

The contractor is due to pay this sum to the employer. How much the employer will receive will depend upon whether the contractor is solvent or not. If he is not, then some proportion only may be available. Any sum arising from the sale of plant which the contractor does not remove cannot be set against the gross in-debtedness shown above, so that the employer gains some benefit in the event of a partial payment only. Plant sales money must be paid in full to the contractor, less only the expenses of sale.

INDEMNITY, INJURY AND INSURANCE

These subjects are linked in that the matters of indemnity under the conditions *include* injury, while insurance is required against most injury.

Indemnity

All indemnity is given only by the contractor to the employer under the express provisions of the conditions, although liability in the opposite direction could arise under the wider law.

	Clause refs
• Liability for statutory fees and charges,	6.2
• although employer reimburses them to contractor	—
• either in contract sum or as an addition	—
• Claims etc. over royalties and patent rights included in contract sum	9
• although those arising by variations, etc. are additions	—
• Injury to persons and property in general	20
• limited by varying considerations of negligence etc. of employer etc. (see next heading)	—
• excludes injury due to	—
• excepted risks	21.3
• perils when employer insures against them	22B, 22C
• otherwise it includes the works themselves	—

Various subsidiary indemnities also occur between contractor and sub-contractors, related to the above.

Injury

Liability for causing injury and bearing the cost of injury sus-tained is related to the law in general, as affected by the indemni-ties under clause 20 outlined above. The major references to injury are given below in relation to contractual liability.

Clause refs

- Materials on site, contractor's liability   16.1
  - unless employer insures   22B, 22C
- Materials off-site, contractor's liability   16.2
- Persons, contractor's liability   20.1
  - unless due to employer's negligence etc.   —
- Property, contractor's liability   20.2
  - provided negligent etc.   —
  - subject to clauses following   —
- Property, contractor not liable for   21.2
  special types of injury
  - in absence of his negligence etc.   —
- Property, contractor not liable over   21.3
  excepted risks
- Work executed and materials on site   22A
  insured by contractor, contractor already
  liable under clause 20.2
- Work executed and materials on site   22B, 22C
  insured by employer, employer liable
  - when injury due to clause 22 perils   —
  - otherwise contractor remains liable   —
    under clause 20.2
- Existing structures and contents insured   22C
  by employer, liability as last
- Work executed and materials on site,   33.1
  employer liable to reimburse contractor
  for war damage
  - should he still require contractor to   —
    continue
  - but in any case employer retains   —
    compensation

Some of the foregoing confirm and some modify the contractor's basic liability under clause 2.1 to 'carry out and complete the Works', which otherwise is obliging him to complete at his own expense whatever injury the works sustain from whatever cause, unless the contract becomes frustrated. The certificate of practical completion under clause 17.1 ends the contractor's liability for injury to the works, as the employer is then entitled to take possession. If partial possession or sectional completion precedes practical completion, liability for the part handed over to the employer passes to him at that time.

Insurance
The insurances required by the conditions are to back up, but not

replace, the indemnities and other liabilities assumed by the parties. Some are required by statute. In the other cases, if the insuring party defaults in taking out or maintaining the insurance, the other party may take it out and counter-charge the first party. No adjustment of the contract sum itself occurs, except when there is a provisional sum.

	Clause refs
• Injury (including death) to persons and to property, insurance provided by contractor	21.1
• over employees etc. to comply with statute	—
• over other persons and property, to be for sums given in appendix	—
• for property, the scope covers works and adjoining property, subject to specific insurances hereafter	—
• Injury to property, probably adjoining and possibly belonging to the employer, but not the works	21.2
• when contractor not negligent	—
• when caused in certain ways	—
• insurance provided by contractor	—
• in joint names of employer and contractor	—
• set against provisional sum in contract bills	—
• Insurance against the excepted risks is not required, by definition	21.3
• Injury to work executed and materials on site	22A
• caused by clause 22 perils	—
• so that (e.g.) theft and vandalism not covered	—
• insurance provided by contractor in joint names of employer and contractor	—
• Same scope as last	22B, 22C
• insurance provided by employer	—
• *not* in joint names	—
• Injury to existing structures and contents	22C
• caused by clause 22 perils	—
• insurance provided by employer	—
• *not* in joint names	—

A comparison of the alternative insurances under clause 22 is given in Chapter 8.

Procedures for reinstatement and settlement under clause 22

The similarities and differences over physical reinstatement and financial settlement under the alternative parts of clause 22 are given in Chapter 8.

CHAPTER 15

FINANCE AND FINALISATION

CONTRACT SUM AND ADJUSTMENT

Contract sum

The contract sum is the consideration from the employer afforded to the contractor in return for his consideration of performing the works. Under the 'entire contract' principle discussed in Chapter 1, it can be adjusted only when the contract permits (see list of provisions below). The main points about it are:

	Clause refs
• Amount is stated in the articles of agreement	—
• It will be identical with the amount on the form of tender (which is *not* a document in the contract), unless there has been a negotiated adjustment between the times of tendering and of accepting the tender	—
• It should be identical with the total of the contract bills. If not, the contract sum will override the other sum and the difference will rank as a non-adjustable 'error'	14.2
• Amount is declared to be non-adjustable	14.2
• even when there are pricing or other arithmetical errors apparent on the face of the contract bills	—
• except when the conditions expressly permit adjustment	—
• Quality and quantity of work represented by the contract sum is to be that in the contract bills	14.1
• adjustment for errors of quantity or description in the contract bills leads to adjustment of the contract sum	2.2.2.2
• contract bills therefore override the contract drawings on the content of the contract sum	—
• architect is to resolve discrepancies	2.3

    between the contract bills and the
    contract drawings
- if this adjusts what is in the contract   —
  bills, the contract sum will be
  adjusted in consequençe
- Adjustments of the contract sum may be   3
  taken into account under interim
  certificates

Adjustments of the contract sum

The following adjustments arise expressly under the conditions
and are referred to in their generality by clause 3:

	Clause refs
- Statutory fees or charges	6.2
- Amending errors in setting out	7
- Cost of inspection and testing	8.3
- Royalties arising out of instructions	9.2
- Variations and provisional sum expenditure	13.7
- Making good defects	17.2
- Ditto	17.3
- Insurance of employer's liability	21.2.3
- Insurance premiums on employer's default	22B.1.3
- Ditto	22C.1.2
- Loss and expense due to disturbance	16.5
- Loss and expense due to antiquities	34.3.3
- Substituted nominated sub-contract amounts	35.24.7
- Expense in obtaining nominated supply goods	36.3.2
- Fluctuations	38.4.4
- Ditto	39.5.4
- Ditto	40.1.1.1

Clause 30.6.2 also falls under clause 3. It gives a list of final
adjustments and again covers all the above, except the two items
out of clauses 35 and 36. In addition this clause covers the adjustment of prime cost sums by the substitution of amounts for
accounts of:

- Contractor
- Nominated sub-contractors
- Nominated suppliers

Clause 15.3 allows for payment to the contractor of loss of credit
for VAT, without falling specifically under clause 3.

Financial adjustments other than by adjustment of contract sum
The following deductions or recoveries may be made by the employer from the adjusted contract sum, but are not taken into account in adjusting it (see 'Example of deductions' hereafter):

	Clause refs
• Work by others on contractor's non-compliance	4.1.2
• Insurance premiums on contractor's default	21.3
• Ditto	22A.2
• Liquidated damages	24.2.1
• Unrecovered costs of substituted sub-contracts	35.24.6

The following adjustments are provided without it being stated how they are to be made, although the method is fairly obvious in each case:

	Clause refs
• Balance after determination by employer	27.4.4
• Balance after determination by contractor	28.2.2
• Reduction of future amounts to recover direct payments to nominated sub-contractors	35.13.5.3
• Payment or allowance of unrecovered costs of substituted sub-contractors	35.18.1.2

The following payments or adjustments are to be made outside the main framework:

	Clause refs
• Statutory tax deduction scheme	31
• VAT agreement	Supplementary provision
• Payment for loss of credit for VAT, no definition of how this is to be made	15.3

Rules for calculating adjustments

• In most cases, the conditions give authority for adjustments but do not lay down details	—
• For loss and expense generally a procedure is given, but not rules for calculation	26
• For loss and expense due to antiquities there is no procedure and there are no rules	34
• Rules are given for	—

- valuation of variations and provisional   13
  sum expenditure
- calculation of fluctuations   38, 39, 40
  - formula method relies heavily on   —
    the formula rules to which it relates

PAYMENTS

Payments show a further modification of the 'entirety' principle, since there is provision for payments on account. They also take in adjustments as covered in the previous section.

Timing of interim payments

Clause refs

- During progress   —
  - regularly, as frequency stated in appendix   30.1.3
    - usually monthly   —
    - until that next after practical completion   —
    - no matter how small the amount   —
  - day of month important if formula   40.2
    fluctuations apply
- After completion   —
  - irregularly, as amounts accrue   —
    - subject to minimum interval of one   30.1.3
      month
      - including when defects made
        good and retention no longer to
        be held   —
    - not subject to this interval   30.7
      - to pay any final amounts to   —
        nominated sub-contractors
    - but at least 28 days before final   —
      cerficate

Main elements of interim payments

- Described as 'value' and including   —
  nominated items
  - as listed in detail below   —
- Work executed, subject to retention   30.2.1
  - as instalments of contract sum   —
    - with additions / omissions for   —
      adjustments of contract sum

- basis of calculation *not* defined —
  - apparently measured rates etc. in contract bills —
  - but caution may be needed until further work gives security to work executed —
- Materials and goods, subject to retention 30.2.1
  - on site —
    - not too early —
    - properly protected —
  - off-site —
    - at architect's discretion —
    - subject to provisos 30.3
  - basis of calculation *not* defined —
    - usually invoice price, if reasonably in line with contract bills —
- Other amounts, not subject to retention 30.2.2, 30.2.3
  - these *include* —
    - fees and premiums —
    - loss and expense —
    - final amounts for nominated sub-contractors —
    - fluctuations, additions or omissions —
  - basis of calculation as may be defined in other authorising clauses —
- Amounts of previous payments are 30.2
  - deducted from total of foregoing —
  - *not* reduced here to allow for any deductions made by employer (see heading hereafter) —

Retention on interim payments
- Purpose, *inferred* from conditions —
  - to pay for making good defects after completion, if contractor does not make good 17.2, 17.3
  - to provide against costs after determination of contractor's employment by employer 27.4
- Not held on some interim amounts 30.2.2, 30.2.3
  - see list under last heading —
  - mostly not held on adjustments of contract sum not representing changes in physical work —

- Status as trust fund   30.5
  - but employer   —
    - retains any interest   —
    - may deduct from releases when   —
      conditions provide
  - divided into   —
    - contractor's retention   —
    - nominated sub-contract retention   —
      - as a whole   —
      - but with amount for each   —
        sub-contractor known
  - separate single banking account to be   —
    maintained
    - for *all* retention   —
    - if contractor or *any* nominated   —
      sub-contractor requests
- Amount of retention   30.4
  - 'the retention percentage' to be 5%
    - unless otherwise in appendix
    - footnote recommends not more
      than 3% for larger contracts
  - proportion of percentage to be held
    - full, before practical completion
    - half, between practical
      completion and making
      good defects
    - none, thereafter   —
  - sectional completion and partial
    possession
    - produce
      - deemed practical completion   —
      - early making good defects   —
    - so that reduction of retention occurs   —
      early for the part(s) concerned
  - early final payment of nominated   30.7
    sub-contractors gives a single stage
    reduction of retention to none

Nominated sub-contractors
- These persons are paid by contractor, but   —
  receive special treatment by employer
  and architect
- Normal payments through contractor   30.2.1.4

- amounts and timing in interim   35.13.1
  certificates decided only by architect
- nominated sub-contractors advised by   35.13.1
  architect of these amounts
- retention separately identified   30.5.2
- time limits for payment by contractor   35.13.2
  prescribed
- architect checks that contractor has made   35.13.3
  payments correctly before issuing next
  interim certificate
  - final payment made ahead of final   30.7
    certificate, allowing a further check   35.17
    - may be early, if employer /   —
      nominated sub-contractor
      agreement in force
- Special direct payments by employer   35.13.5
  - possible only if contractor has   —
    defaulted over a previous amount
    - *not* over a current amount, even if   —
      future default likely
  - obligatory if employer/nominated   —
    sub-contractor agreement in force
    - optional otherwise   —
  - made at same time (usually) as equal   —
    amount deducted from contractor's
    payment
  - employer not obliged to pay direct   —
    more than can deduct
    - if necessary therefore shares out   —
      direct payments, usually
      proportionately
  - procedure ceases upon contractor's   —
    insolvency
- Only recognised exception to foregoing: NSC/4, NSC/4a
  set-off under nominated sub-contracts
  - strictly limited in scope   —
  - subject to right of adjudication   —

Final payment
(see 'Architect' and 'Contract sum and adjustment')
- Stated as due in final certificate   30.8
  - by setting down   —
    - contract sum as adjusted   —
    - amounts already certified   —

- difference as balance due, either —
  way
- amount does *not* include —
  - VAT dealt with by supplementary —
    agreement
  - effect of deductions which employer —
    may make/have made from it
- Based upon final account embodying all   30.6
  adjustments of contract sum
  - procedure   —
    - contractor may attend and take   13.6
      notes of variation measurements
    - contractor sends architect/quantity   30.6.1
      surveyor all necessary documents
    - quantity surveyor values in   13.5
      accordance with the conditions
    - quantity surveyor sends statement   30.6.1, 30.6.3
      of final valuations etc. to contractor
      - strictly, does not cover all   30.6.2
        adjustments
    - no requirement to agree final   —
      account given
  - prerequisites   —
    - instructions leading to adjustment   4.1
      - confirmation of any not in writing   4.3
      - establishment of any 'deemed'
        instructions (see list under
        'Architect')
    - other contractual authority, e.g.   —
      over fluctuations
    - completion of any arbitration   —
      already proceeding
- Conclusive, subject to   30.9
  - fraud   —
  - error in computations   —
  - arbitration on final certificate itself   —
    - this allows for lack of agreement of
      final account

Deductions by employer
- There are several instances in which   —
  employer may counter-claim against
  contractor
  - by deduction from amounts due, or by   —
    action for debt

- to reduce amounts certified by —
  architect
- while architect must *not* deduct them —
  in arriving at certified amounts (see
  next example)
- These may be deductions from interim or —
  final amounts
- These therefore rank as adjustments —
  other than of contract sum (see list under
  'Contract sum and adjustment')

Example of deductions for direct payments to nominated sub-contractors

This takes the key figures for two certificates in the middle of a
contract period, giving alternative versions of events according to
whether there is enough to pay the sub-contractor the amount by
which the contractor has defaulted or not.

Certificate 10

Total amount net of retention	320,000
Less amounts of certs. 1–9	270,000
Amount due	£50,000

When this certificate is being prepared, it is discovered that the
contractor has failed to pay nominated sub-contractor 'A' the
amount included in certificate 9. Two versions of this amount are
used for illustrative purposes.

	Not enough available	*Enough available*
Amount not paid to NSC 'A'	£60,000	£40,000
Payments by employer in respect of cert. 10:		
To NSC 'A'	50,000	40,000
(leaving deficit of £10,000)		
To contractor	Nil	10,000
Total as due	£50,000	£50,000

Certificate 11

Total amount net of retention including amount not paid as shown above, but not next amount	340,000
Amount for NSC 'B' net of retention	20,000
Total net	£360,000
Less amounts of certs. 1–10	320,000
Amount due	£40,000

Assuming the 'not enough available' version and further default, the employer could be faced with the problem of rationing payments again. A 'fair and reasonable' approach to this might be:

		Not paid	Direct payments now
NSC 'A'	Cert. 9	10,000	10,000
	Cert. 10	20,000	15,000
NSC 'C'	Cert. 10	20,000	15,000
Totals due/available		£50,000	£40,000

This allocation of amounts uses a 'queuing' system, that is it pays the amounts longest outstanding first. It then shares out the remainder proportionately to what is owed. Not only does it not pay anything to NSC 'B' (because the contractor has yet to default over him), but it effectively takes his amount from the contractor to help pay the others. This does *not* relieve the contractor of his responsibility to pay NSC 'B'. He has had all the amounts and is behind! Only if the amount for NSC 'B' is a release of retention is the employer unable to touch it in this way, as he has it in trust for the sub-contractor.

Assuming the 'enough available' version and no further default, what the architect should *not* do in preparing his certificate 11 is to deal with amounts as follows:

Incorrect certificate 11

Total amount net of retention		360,000
Less amounts of certs. 1–10, as paid, i.e.		
Totals	320,000	
Direct payment	40,000	280,000
Amount due		£80,000

This calculation would pay back to the contractor the amount deducted from certificate 10 on behalf of NSC 'A'. The amounts certified should always be shown, whatever deductions may have been made by the employer in accordance with the conditions.

Example of retention allocations at partial possession during a contract

No attempt is made to follow the standard layout for an interim valuation in preparation for a certificate. Partial possession of the subsidiary building has occurred.

	Subsidiary building	Main building
Work as contract bills	20,000	80,000
Variations, including daywork	1,000	3,000
NSC 'A' (paid in full)	—	—
NSC 'B'	2,000	8,000
Profit at 5% on all amounts for NSCs 'A' and 'B', above and below,		
i.e. on £5,400 say	300	—
i.e. on £19,500 say	—	1,000
Materials on site	—	4,000
Amounts subject to retention	£23,300	£96,000
NSC 'A' (see above)	3,000	10,000
Fees and charges	—	500
Approximate value of relevant part	£26,300	—
for clause 18 purposes		
Loss and expense of contractor	2,000	3,000
Loss and expense of NSC 'B'	300	1,000
Fluctuations clause 39 of contractor	2,000	6,000
Ditto NSC 'B'	100	500
	£30,700	£117,000
Subsidiary building transfer		30,700
Gross total of valuation		£147,700
Less retention 2½% on £23,300	600	
5% on £96,000	4,800	5,400
		£142,300
Less previous valuations		124,600
Current valuation		£17,700

These figures show or suggest several points of note:
- Retention on the subsidiary building has been halved.
- The balance of retention on this building may be cleared before or after the first reduction of retention on the main building according to progress on that building or the clearing of defects on the subsidiary building.
- Most of the amounts carrying no retention never carry any, under the contract provisions. The exception is the amount for NSC 'A' mentioned below.
- Nominated sub-contractors
  - NSC 'A' has had all retention released in one stage, in accordance with clause 35.17. The amount still needs to be included in the total for purposes of clause 18.
  - While the various nominated amounts are not all subject to retention, the contractor's profit upon them is.
  - The total retention shown must be split into the two elements of contractor's and nominated sub-contract retentions, to satisfy the trust fund requirements.
  - Each nominated sub-contractor is to be informed of the amount included in the certificate issued on his account and of the amount of retention held.

COMPLETION AND SETTLEMENT

Physical completion
See 'Standard pattern of progress' under 'Progress and disturbance'.

Financial settlement
See 'Final payment' under 'Payments'.

Final certificate

	Clause refs
• Issued by architect within 3 months of latest of	30.8
• end of defects liability period	—
• completion of making good defects	—
• receipt of final account documents from contractor	—
• Nominated sub-contractors to be informed, because it indicates when their liabilities will end in the future	30.8
• Effect is to end contract, subject to residual liabilities	—

- Conclusive evidence in arbitration or   30.9.1
  court action
  - over physical work   —
    - when this to be to architect's   —
      reasonable satisfaction, so that
      - contractor released from liability   —
      - architect may become liable   —
        under his conditions of
        engagement for these aspects
    - but not otherwise, so that   —
      - contractor remains liable for any   —
        breach due to non-compliance
        with express standards required
        by contract documents
      - contractor *usually* remains liable   —
        for *most* of work until the
        limitations period expires
  - that all terms requiring financial   —
    adjustment have been observed
    - unless there is accident or error over   —
      quantity or money
      - in any supporting calculations   —
      - this therefore extends back to the   —
        contract bills
- Conclusiveness is subject to   —
  - fraud   —
  - proceedings (see next heading)   —

Proceedings
- These may take two forms   —
  - arbitration (see next heading)   Art. 5
  - court action   —
    - *not* precluded by the provisions   —
      given for arbitration
    - may therefore be used   —
      - instead of arbitration   —
      - by one party unilaterally   —
      - at any time during the contract,   —
        whereas arbitration is restricted
- Proceedings affect the final certificate   —
  - if concluded before final certificate   —
    issued, this must take account of them
  - if under way when final certificate   30.9.2
    issued
    - final certificate conclusive *except* on   —

subject-matter of proceedings and
subject to outcome, or
- final certificate becomes conclusive   —
  if proceedings lapse completely for
  any 12 months after its issue
- if either party commences proceedings   30.9.3
  within 14 days of issue of final
  certificate
  - final certificate becomes conclusive   —
    except on subject-matter of
    proceedings and subject to outcome
- otherwise later proceedings   —
  - subject to conclusiveness of final   —
    certificate on its subject-matter, and
  - can be pursued only over other   —
    matters on which final certificate *not*
    conclusive
- Provision of clauses over loss and   26, 27, 28
  expense and determination is 'without
  prejudice to'
  - and therefore does not preclude   —
    - arbitration, which in turn does not   —
      preclude
      - court action   —
  - these may be used instead of or as well   —
    as one another
- Article 5 defines 'the proper law'   —
  (including over arbitration) as
  - that of England, unless article is   —
    amended
    - irrespective of nationality,   —
      residence or location
      considerations

Arbitration

- Arbitration governed generally by   —
  Arbitration Acts 1950–79 in England
  and Wales and other legislation
  elsewhere
- It requires agreement of both parties to   —
  enter upon it, as to
  - subject-matter of arbitration   —
  - person(s) acting as arbitrator(s)   —
- Article 5 gives agreement   Art. 5
  - over subject-matter   —

- cast very widely to include   —
  - interpretation of contract   —
  - certificates, decisions, consents   —
    etc. of either party or architect
  - but to exclude tax matters and   —
    (under local authorities edition) fair
    wages
  - to appointment of single arbitrator   —
    - agreed between parties   —
    - or appointed by RIBA   —
  - that nominated sub-contractor or   —
    nominated supplier may be joined in
    same reference if subject-matter
    common
  - that reference not to be opened until   —
    after practical completion or its
    equivalent, except
    - on a few critical issues, or   —
    - by agreement   —
- Arbitrator has considerable power   —
  - over scope and method of enquiry   —
    - but limited to matters referred   —
  - to refer matters of law to the courts   —
  - award final   —
    - without appeal in general   —
      therefore, but
    - subject to compliance with   —
      Arbitration Acts

TABLE OF CASES

These cases are of interest in relation to the forms of contract discussed in this book. Some are related to earlier editions of these forms, dealing with provisions that may be unchanged or that may have been modified in current editions. Other cases were decided on non-standard forms. All cases may be consulted to deepen the legal background of the commentary, but the specific wording of current editions may lead to different legal decisions based on the same underlying principles.

Cases are grouped under headings and followed by notes, to indicate their salient features for present purposes only. Cases are referenced where possible to the readily available Building Law Reports (BLR).

ARBITRATION

Scott v. *Avery* (1856)
Decision that a contract (not building) precluded initial court action: *not* so in standard forms
Dawnays Ltd v. *F. G. Minter Ltd and Trollope and Colls Ltd* (1971) 1 BLR 16
Court action allowed ahead of arbitration to help cash flow
James Miller and Partners Ltd v. *Whitworth Estates (Manchester) Ltd* (1970)
Whether proper law of contract was English or Scottish and relation to arbitration

DOCUMENTATION AND MEASUREMENT

Brightside Kilpatrick Engineering Services v. *Mitchell Construction (1973) Ltd* (1975) 1 BLR 62
Difficulties in importing main contract terms into sub-contract
Williams v. *Fitzmaurice* (1858)
Discrepancy between drawings and specification in no-quantities contract
English Industrial Estates Corporation v. *George Wimpey and Co. Ltd* (1973)

Printed conditions prevail under JCT forms
J. Crosby and Sons Ltd v. *Portland Urban District Council* (1967) 5
BLR 121
Choice of alternative specifications by engineer and instructions to
suspend work
Neodox Ltd v. *The Borough of Swinton and Pendlebury* (1958)
Reasonableness of delay in issue of information by engineer and of
instructions over working methods

DELAY AND LIQUIDATED DAMAGES

(Some cases under 'Certificates and payments' also relate to this
theme and to the wider question of deductions from sums due)
Re Newman, ex parte Capper (1876)
Distinction between liquidated damages and penalty
Law v. *Redditch Local Board* (1892)
Terms and amounts for several provisions for liquidated damages
held to be unambiguous and reasonable
Davis Contractors Ltd v. *Fareham Urban District Council* (1956)
Extreme delay: effects borne by employer, cost by contractor
Peake Construction (Liverpool) Ltd v. *McKinney Foundations Ltd*
(1970) 1 BLR 111
Sub-contractor's defective work and dilatoriness by employer in
making decisions, affecting damages and fluctuations
Trollope and Colls Ltd v. *North West Metropolitan Regional Hospital Board* (1973) 9 BLR 60
Effect of delay in one phase of contract on costs in a later phase;
adequacy of express contract terms

DISTURBANCE, DETERMINATION AND LOSS AND EXPENSE

Hadley v. *Baxendale* (1854)
Principle of direct loss
Saint Line Ltd v. *Richardsons, Westgarth and Co.* (1940)
Direct loss, including overheads and profit as recoverable if
'direct' loss
F. G. Minter Ltd v. *Welsh Health Technical Services Organisation*
(1980) 13 BLR 1
Direct loss due to disturbance of progress, with delayed reimbursement
Wraight Ltd v. *P. H. and T. Holdings Ltd* (1968) 13 BLR 26
Direct loss by contractor on his determination

Hounslow London Borough Council v. *Twickenham Garden Developments Ltd* (1971) 7 BLR 81
Determination by employer, with a doubted decision over site repossession

INJURY TO PERSONS AND PROPERTY AND INDEMNITIES

Buckinghamshire County Council v. *Y. J. Lovell and Son Ltd* (1956)
Indemnity of contractor existed only when he was negligent; here he was liable
Gold v. *Patman and Fotheringham Ltd* (1958)
Indemnity of contractor existed only when he was negligent; here he was not liable
English Industrial Estates Corporation v. *George Wimpey and Co. Ltd* (1973)
Majority view that special conditions inserted were to apply in favour of employer in actual circumstances of progress, despite general principle that printed conditions were to prevail under the contract form

INSOLVENCY OF CONTRACTOR AND TITLE TO GOODS

Re Wilkinson, ex parte Fowler (1905)
Direct payments to firms after insolvency of contractor
Re Tout and Finch Ltd (1954)
Direct payments to firms after insolvency of contractor
Re Fox, ex parte Oundle and Thrapston Rural District Council v. *The Trustee* (1948)
Matters of reputed ownership
Aluminium Industrie Vaassen BV v. *Romalpa Aluminium Ltd* (1976)
Defective title to goods on payment to main contractor
Humberside County Council v. *Dawber Williamson Roofing Ltd* (1979)
Defective title to goods on payment to main contractor

SUPPLIERS AND SUB-CONTRACTORS

Westminster Corporation v. *J. Jarvis and Sons Ltd and Another* (1969)

Delay 'on the part of' a nominated sub-contractor differs from delay 'caused by' such a person, affecting JCT arrangements extensively
Gloucestershire County Council v. *Richardson* (1969)
Contractor not liable for matters excluded by supplier and allowed so in contract of supply by architect
Young and Marten Ltd v. *McManus Childs Ltd* (1969) 9 BLR 77
Terms similar to those for a sale of goods implied in a contract for work and materials; this case contrasts with that immediately above, which is referred to *in extenso* under the present case in BLR

CERTIFICATES, PAYMENTS AND SET-OFF

Tharsis Sulphur and Copper Company v. *McElroy and Sons* (1878)
Interim payments did not establish right to final payment without formal instructions
R. B. Burden Ltd v. *Swansea Corporation* (1957)
Contractor not entitled to determine for undercertification, as distinct from interference by employer
Dawnays Ltd v. *F. G. Minter Ltd and Trollope and Colls Ltd* (1971) 1 BLR 16
Dubiety over set-off for damages for delay when certificate lacking
Gilbert Ash (Northern) Ltd v. *Modern Engineering (Bristol) Ltd* (1974) 1 BLR 73
Dubiety over set-off for damages for delay when certificate lacking, probably running contrary to last case
Killby and Gayford v. *Selincourt* (1973)
Employer not to withhold payment on certificate, but to question apparently high amount with architect, this contrasting with detail of last case
Token Construction Co. Ltd v. *Charlton Estates Ltd* (1973) 1 BLR 48
Employer not to deduct liquidated damages without formal certificate from architect, rather than an opinion

CERTIFICATES AND APPROVALS

Newton Abbot Development Co. Ltd v. *Stockman Bros* (1931)
Satisfaction of local authority with work did not relieve contractor of satisfying employer over specified quality
East Ham Corporation v. *Bernard Sunley and Sons Ltd* (1966)
Contractor's liability for latent defects in relation to the architect's

BIBLIOGRAPHY

LEGAL PRINCIPLES AND CASES

Outline of the Law of Contract and Tort. G. G. G. Robb and John P. Brookes (Estates Gazette Ltd)
Construction Law. John Uff (Sweet and Maxwell)
Law and Practice of Building Contracts. D. Keating (Sweet and Maxwell)
Building Law Reports. A series issued at intervals (George Godwin)

THE STANDARD FORMS

The Standard Forms of Building Contract. Sir Derek Walker-Smith and Howard A. Close (Charles Knight and Co.)
A New Approach to the 1980 Standard Form of Building Contract. Glyn P. Jones (Construction Press)
Building Contracts: a Practical Guide. Dennis F. Turner (George Godwin)
Practice Notes. Issued from time to time by the Joint Contracts Tribunal (available from RIBA, NFBTE and RICS)
Articles in various journals from time to time cover topical aspects and recent cases.

INDEX

This index has been structured in the usual way, but takes account of the following:

- No items have been included for
  - contract forms listed in Chapter 2
  - synopses in Chapters 3–11
  - Chapter 12 in its entirety
  - Table of Cases
- Chapters 13–15 consist almost entirely of a close structure of contract themes and may be used as a non-alphabetical entry into earlier chapters by means of the clause references
- There are therefore entries for the *main* constituents of Chapters 13–15, while Chapter 12 lists their sections in order and also in relation to the chapters in Part 2.
- The full range of contents of Part 1 and 2 are otherwise covered, and in particular elements not emphasized in Chapters 13–15.